$\mathscr{B}$E FRUITFUL AND MULTIPLY

*B*E FRUITFUL AND MULTIPLY

What the Bible Says
About Having Children

NANCY CAMPBELL

VISION FORUM MINISTRIES
SAN ANTONIO, TEXAS

"Where there is no vision, the people perish."

Vision Forum Ministries
4719 Blanco Rd., San Antonio, Texas 78212
www.visionforum.org

ISBN 0-9724173-5-4

Cover Design by Al Mendenhall
Typesetting by Jeremy M. Fisher

PRINTED IN THE UNITED STATES OF AMERICA

CONTENTS

ℱOREWORD

"Be thou the mother of thousands of millions,
and let thy seed possess the gate..."

Can you imagine attending a wedding where families and friends offered the above blessing to a new bride? Yet these words of encouragement, once offered to Rebekah on the advent of her marriage to Isaac (Genesis 24:60), beautifully communicate the heart of God's command to Christian husbands and wives that they be exceedingly fruitful and raise children who will influence all of culture and society for the glory of God.

There is no escaping the fact that the Bible is dogmatically pro-child. Scripture declares unapologetically that the birth of many children is a source of blessing, that a key reason for marriage is to bring forth many children for the glory of God, and that parents should actively seek such blessings.

The Bible begins with a mandate for conception. The first great commission given to man was to "be fruitful and multiply." This commission to bring forth many children for the glory of God and through them to subdue the earth was first given to

Adam and Eve and their progeny, and was later renewed to Noah in the days following the Great Flood, and remains our standard for today—a fact that is clear from the affirmation by the Lord Jesus of the Genesis marriage mandate upon which the fruitfulness and dominion commission rests (Matthew 19:4-6).

But there is more: The Bible abounds with examples of people of diverse economic backgrounds who were considered blessed to have many children. There appears to be no relationship whatsoever between the economic status of a family and the mandate to bring forth children. Rich and poor alike are to have many children for the glory of God and to recognize that the same God who gives life is also able to provide for the life He brings into the world. In fact, in the biblical model, large numbers of children not only increase the spiritual blessing of the family, but potentially increase the financial strength of the family as well, as parents and children join in unison to contribute to the economy of the household.

In contrast with our modern society which promotes barrenness, population control, and abortion, the Bible consistently associates the inability to conceive with sorrow, a decrease in a nation's population with judgment, and the careless and harmful treatment of babies with paganism and witchcraft.

The Bible is not silent on the issue of conception control. At least four patterns and precepts are relevant: First, under the Mosaic law, complete abstinence was the natural consequence of the ceremonial uncleanness during the season of a woman's menstruation or after the birth of a child. Second, the apostle Paul instructed husbands and wives that they may choose to exercise complete abstinence for a season of self-examination. Third, Scripture offers the controversial but relevant passage in which we learn that Onan, now married to his brother's widow, is struck dead by the Lord for practicing a form of conception control, with the goal of preventing children who will bear his brother's name.

Finally, in the Bible, there is no separation of life from love. Sometimes it is the sovereign will of God for Him to permanently close the womb of a woman, and when He does this, we must accept in faith His will. (Ultimately, the Lord does this for all women through the aging process. But the Scripture offers no refuge to the idea that man may deliberately separate the "life" component from the "love" component of the holy union between man and woman. In fact, in the context of a broader discussion on perversion in Romans 1, we learn that God is not pleased when people do that which is "against nature" with their bodies for the purpose of sexual gratification. The common denominator in all acts of perversion is that they go against the natural design of God for our bodies, they separate life from biblical love, and they attack the procreative goals of the institution of marriage. Thus, an argument could be made that the modern birth control ethic, with its vision for deliberately separating life from love and altering the natural functions of the body, is yet another form of selfish unbiblical gratification which should be condemned.

It is fair to say that for six thousand years of earth history, the unanimous sentiment of Hebrew and Christian culture was opposition to birth control, support for conception within marriage, and recognition of the blessing of children. Of course, forms of birth control have been with man since the ancients, but it has only been in the twentieth century, with the influence of evolutionism and eugenics, that Christians have publicly embraced the notion of child prevention.

The point is this: The Bible is enthusiastically pro-childbirth, and what it does say of relevance to the issue of conception control is comprehensively negative. There are no clear patterns, precepts, or principles found in the Bible which seem to give any leeway to the idea that couples should alter their bodies and cut off their seed. Until recently, this was the universally accepted principle of Christian culture.

This is why Christians who advocate conception control have a whopping task: The burden of proof rests on them (not those of us who argue for the normative and plain teaching of Scripture) to prove from Scripture alone that God is pleased with us altering our bodies and thwarting children from coming into the world. It is not enough to argue from the "penumbras and emanations" of the Scripture, or to hope that there is a stewardship principle which would support the practice of cutting off the seed. One must actively prove from clear patterns, precepts, and principles of Scripture that child prevention is part of the jurisdiction over which man may lawfully exercise stewardship. This is an important point because all sorts of wrongs can be argued on the basis of "stewardship." The relevant question is this: "do we have the jurisdiction and authority to thwart children?"

The great tragedy of our day is that the Church has been swept up in the birth control ethic, with its selfish quest for convenience, comfort, and the self-deceiving vision of the individual's control over his own destiny. The fact is that we have lost our love for children and our vision to be fruitful, multiply, and have dominion over the earth. The results have been devastating.

In fact, many Christians are unaware that they are not only engaging in an unbiblical practice of preventing "blessings," but that some of the very practices they embrace have abortifacient consequences. How sad to think that someday we will get to Heaven and learn of the untold millions of children that were inadvertently aborted by their Christian parents—all because of lack of faith and ignorance. "My people are destroyed for a lack of knowledge."

I have a simple thesis: Hollywood is not the primary problem in the battle for our families. Neither do Wall Street, nor Madison Avenue, have any more power over our households than that which we grant to them. The problem is not the media. The problem is not Planned Parenthood. The problem is not the "liberal elite." The problem is us.

We are the problem. And judgment must begin with us. As long as we continue to abort our babies, or cut off our seed, or abandon our children to the world, we can never expect blessing and joy within our households, let alone our culture. As long as we view children as a burden, we will not experience the victory of multi-generational faithfulness. Judgment begins first in the House of God. That means us.

Nothing short of a fundamental switch in paradigms will do. We must transform our thinking and our lives such that we, of all people, communicate through our choices, our words, and our families that we love children and view them as God's chosen tool for building the Church and populating the world with future warriors who will dedicate their lives to keep covenant with God and thrash the works of the Devil. We must crave a godly seed. We must actively seek to bring forth legions of children for the glory of God. We must be willing to bless future mothers with the very words given to Rebekah: "May you be the mother of thousands of millions, and may your seed possess the gate."

It is for the perpetuation of this glorious vision that Vision Forum Ministries is pleased to publish this important study guide by Nancy Campbell. For many decades, Mrs. Campbell has served her husband at home and through her Titus 2 ministry to Christian women promoting virtuous womanhood. She and her husband bring to this discussion a wealth of rich insight from God's Word which we hope will inspire you to search the Scripture diligently on the issue of trusting our sovereign God for the birth of children. It is my prayer that in years to come, we will have the privilege of meeting many hundreds, if not thousands of children, who would not have been born, but for the wonderful new vision for fruitfulness inspired by this thought-provoking study guide.

Doug Phillips
Vision Forum Ministries

*I*NTRODUCTION

What are God's Purposes for Marriage and the Family?

The traditional wedding vows give the following three reasons for marriage:

Firstly, it was ordained for the increase of mankind, according to the will of God and that children might be brought up in the fear and nurture of the Lord, and to the praise of His holy name.

Secondly, it was ordained in order that the natural instinct and affections, implanted by God, should be hallowed and directed aright; that those who are called of God to this holy estate, should continue therein in pureness of living.

Thirdly, it was ordained for the mutual society, help and comfort that the one ought to have of the other, both in prosperity, and adversity.

I believe the Word of God gives three further reasons:

Fourthly, we need one another to help fulfill God's command to manage God's Creation.

Fifthly, it is a powerful force for effective prayer.

Sixthly, it was ordained to portray to the world a picture of the relationship of Christ and His church.

The above reasons are all part of the marriage relationship, and all part of God's beautiful plan for marriage. Each one is as equally important as the other. As we shall see, these are not man's principles, but God's. Look at the Scriptures as we check each one, from last to first.

To Portray to the World a Picture of Christ and His Church:

Ephesians 5:21-33, "This is a great mystery: but I speak concerning Christ and the church." This greatest exhortation on marriage reveals that marriage is the picture of Christ and His church. If any of these reasons could be more important than the other, this would have to be the reason. Marriage is the outworking on earth of the picture of this glorious theological truth. What a magnificent reason for marriage. This outworking takes a lifetime.

It can only be accomplished by allowing the Holy Spirit to daily have His way in our lives by allowing the fruit of the Holy Spirit—love, joy, peace, long-suffering, gentleness, goodness, faithfulness, meekness, and self-control; by having the same mind that Jesus had, who did not hold on to His own rights, but humbled Himself and became obedient to the death of the cross; by having a tender and soft heart to one another; and by giving up every selfish motive and living only for the other. This is the true picture of marriage.

To Have Unity in Prayer:

Jesus said in Matthew 18:19-20, "That if two of you shall agree on earth as touching anything that they shall ask, it shall be done for them of my Father which is in heaven. For where two or three are gathered together in my name, there am I in the midst of them." When two hearts unite as one to pray, heaven unleashes mighty blessings upon the earth. This is a great privilege of the marriage union. In Acts chapter 2, we read how the Holy Spirit fell when they were all "with one accord." The oneness of spirit in marriage is a powerful weapon of prayer to God and a powerful force against the enemy.

To Take Dominion Together over God's Creation:

Genesis 1:28, "God said unto them, Be fruitful and multiply and replenish the earth, and subdue it: and have dominion over the fish of the sea, and over the fowl of the air, and over every living thing that moveth upon the earth." This is a big task that God has given to husbands and wives and their families. We cannot accomplish this task individually. We do it together as husband and wife with the help of our growing family.

To Enjoy Companionship Together:

God planned marriage for the purpose of companionship, togetherness, and for husband and wife to help and comfort one another. Genesis 2:18-24, "And the Lord God said, It is not good that the man should be alone; I will make him an help meet for him." Proverbs 5:18, "Rejoice with the wife of thy youth." Read also Deuteronomy 24:5; Proverbs 2:17; Malachi 2:14; Ephesians 5:21-33.

To Enjoy Sexual Unity in the Holy Estate of Marriage:

Hebrews 13:4, "Marriage is honorable in all, and the bed undefiled: but whoremongers and adulterers God will judge." In the confinement of the marriage union, God has created the sexual union for the enjoyment, pleasure, and the delight of man. The blessedness of the marriage bed is hallowed, but outside of marriage, God calls it sin. Further Scripture references to read: Genesis 39:9; Exodus 20:12; Proverbs 5:18,19; 6:27-33; Malachi 2:14; 1 Corinthians 6:18; 7:1-5.

Each one of the above truths are important and are very much part of God's perfect design for marriage. Understanding the truth of each one is necessary to walk in the fullness of God's vision for family. Many books have been written about the second, third, fourth, fifth, and sixth reasons. What about the first reason, "It was ordained for the increase of mankind?" This is rarely spoken about in the church. Is this also Scriptural? Is this a divine mandate from God? Or is it something on which we can make our own decision?

Because this aspect is seldom, if ever, preached about, we are going to concentrate on what God says on this point in this book.

To answer this, we will need to look at the Scriptures. We do not want man's ideas. We want to know what God says. As you go through this book, check every Scripture. Search the Word of God for yourself. Do it with an open and soft heart before the Lord. Do it with a heart that wants to hear God's heartbeat, rather than the humanistic voices in society today. Do it with a heart that is quick to obey the Word of the Lord.

At the end of each chapter, questions are given. These can be used for...

1. Group discussion where this book is used for group Bible studies; or

2. For your personal challenge and meditation in your quiet time. In this case, provision is given for you to write down your thoughts. I would earnestly encourage you to do this. It is the revelation of the Word of God that quickens truth to our hearts and this revelation only comes as we *wait* on God and *meditate* upon His precepts.

You may prefer to read through the book first, opening up your heart to God's revelation and truth. Then pick it up the second time to look up every Scripture and answer the questions. Don't miss out on answering the questions, as they provide many more Scriptures for you to study and meditate upon.

We can only walk in obedience to God's Laws as we receive faith to walk in them. We receive this faith by the knowledge and understanding of the Word of God in our hearts. Therefore, it is important to search the Word of God and let the Word of Christ dwell in us richly. Romans 10:17 says, "Faith comes by hearing, and hearing by the word of God."

May the cry of our hearts be the cry of David. In Psalm 25:4-5 he cries out, "Show me *thy* ways, O LORD; teach me *thy* paths. Lead me in *thy* truth, and teach me: for thou art the God of my salvation; on *thee* do I wait all the day" (emphasis added). There are many voices in the world today. There are many ways that we can go. Different doctrines are preached across the body of Christ. In the midst of all the confusion, we must cry out for God to show us His ways.

The rest of Psalm 25 reveals to whom God will show His ways. God will reveal His truth to those who:

1. Have a meek and humble spirit. Verse 9 says, "The meek will he guide in judgment: and the meek will he teach His way." We cannot hold on in stubbornness to our pre-conceived ideas or traditions. We need to keep a humble spirit that is quick to hear the voice of the Lord. God says in Isaiah 66:2, "But to this man will I look, even to him that is poor, and of a contrite spirit, and trembleth at my word."

2. Walk in the fear of the Lord. Verses 12 and 14 say, "What man is he that feareth the Lord? him shall he teach in the way that he shall choose." and "The secret of the Lord is with them that fear Him; and He will show them His covenant."

The King James Version or the Revised Authorised Version is used in this book, except where otherwise stated. It is the translation of choice, though I have included on occasion other translations and Scripture paraphrases for the purpose of amplification and comparison.

May God bless you and may He lead us all into His truth and His ways.

Nancy Campbell
Primm Springs, Tennessee

CHAPTER 1

⒯HE FIRST COMMANDMENT: BE FRUITFUL AND MULTIPLY

The very first recorded words that man ever heard from the mouth of God were these: "Be fruitful, and multiply, and replenish the earth, and subdue it: and have dominion over the fish of the sea, and over the fowl of the air, and over every living thing that moveth upon the earth" (Genesis 1: 27-28). This was the first commandment that God gave to mankind, so it must be important. Isn't it strange that we seek to obey God's other commandments, but many of us refuse to obey the very first commandment?

What do these words mean in Hebrew?

"Be fruitful"	*parah*	to bear fruit, to bring forth, to increase
"multiply"	*rabah*	to increase exceedingly, to be many, to be abundant

| "replenish" | *male* | to fill up the world to |
| | | overflowing |

Matthew Henry comments on this Scripture, "Pronouncing blessing upon them in virtue of which their posterity should extend to the utmost corners of the earth and continue to the utmost period of time. Fruitfulness and increase depend upon the blessing of God."

After the flood, God re-stated these words to Noah and his family. And in case Noah did not think it was too important, He repeated them twice, saying, "Be ye fruitful, and multiply; bring forth *abundantly* in the earth..." (Genesis 9:1,7, emphasis added). God repeated this command again to Israel in Genesis 35:11. We can find no place in Scripture where God rescinds this command. The law of "the first mention" is important in understanding the Word of God. When God says something the first time, He lays a foundation for that truth. He will build upon it through the rest of His Word, but He will never deviate from the first principle. How could we trust a God who changes His mind halfway through His written Word? How could we trust a Bible that says one thing at the beginning and then changes the doctrine halfway through? No, God's words are changeless. They are for a thousand generations. The words of the Lord are "as silver tried in a furnace of earth, purified seven times" (Psalm 12:6). And Psalm 33:11 says, "The counsel of the Lord stands forever, the plans of His heart to all generations." The principles and commands that God gave us to live out on this earth were planned in the eternal realm before they were released to us. When God gave them to us, they were refined and purified to be workable for every generation and every nation.

THE PURPOSE

Jeremiah 29:6 says, "Take ye wives, and beget sons and daughters; and take wives for your sons, and give your daughters to husbands, that they may bear sons and daughters; that ye may be increased there, and not diminished." The Word of God states in this Scripture that the reason God wants us to marry is that we may bear sons and daughters! God wants many children. The Living Bible paraphrases the Scripture this way, "Marry and have children, and then find mates for them and have many grandchildren. Multiply! Don't dwindle away!"

The Good News Bible offers this amplification of Genesis 1:28 when it says, "Have many children, so that your descendants will live all over the earth and bring it under their control."

In Romans 7:4, Paul uses the illustration of marriage to show how we are to bring forth fruit unto God. The inference in this Scripture is that fruitfulness is the obvious expectation and outcome of marriage—"that ye should be married to another, even to him who is raised from the dead, that we should bring forth fruit unto God." God's intention for the marriage union is that "we should bring forth fruit."

It is interesting that this was the first command God gave to marriage.

He did not say, "I want you to spend the beginning years of your marriage getting to know one another first, then you'll be ready to start a family."

He did not say, "I want you to spend time together, travel, fulfill all your plans and aspirations, then begin your family."

He did not say, "I want you both to work until you have enough money to purchase your own home and accumulate the material possessions you need, then I want you to be fruitful."

No, His first command was, "Be fruitful and multiply."

When the question is asked in Malachi 2:14-15 regarding what God wants from our marriage, His immediate reply is, "I want godly offspring."

THE GENESIS CHARGE

It is interesting that this first commandment is called the Genesis Charge. Scripture says in Psalm 8:6, "Thou madest him to have dominion over the works of thy hands; thou hast put all things under his feet." The Message Bible amplifies this Psalm this way: "You put us in charge of your hand-crafted world, repeated to us your Genesis charge." What was the Genesis Charge? It is repeated from Genesis 1:28, "And God blessed them, and God said unto them, Be fruitful, and multiply, and replenish the earth, and subdue it; and have dominion over the fish of the sea, and over the fowl of the air and over every living thing that moveth upon the earth." Isn't this a great name for this first command? Notice that it is a "charge," not just an option. This could be a good answer to those who are negative about having children. You can smile sweetly and say, "I'm obeying the Genesis Charge!"

INHABIT THE EARTH

God is interested in filling the earth and populating eternity. "But," you say, "what about the population explosion?" Let's examine this in the light of Scripture and current studies. It is foreign to God's mind. He wants the earth to be filled! Remember we found that the word "replenish" means to "fill up the world to overflowing." And contrary to the scare tactics of the would-be population controllers, there is still plenty of room on this earth.

Genesis 9:19, "These are the three sons of Noah: and of them was the whole earth overspread."

Psalm 80:8-11, speaking of Israel, says, "You have brought a vine out of Egypt; You have cast out the nations, and planted it, You prepared room for it, and caused it to take deep root, and it filled the land."

Isaiah 27:5, "He shall cause them that come of Jacob to take root and fill the face of the world with fruit."

Isaiah 45:18, "For thus saith the Lord that created the heavens, God Himself that formed the earth and made it; He hath established it, He created it not in vain, He formed it to be inhabited; I am the Lord and there is none else."

Who are we going to listen to—God, or the population pessimists who have no trust in God? If you have driven from the west coast to the east of America, you will know that most of this great land is still uninhabited. Here are just a few quotes that expose their deceiving propaganda:

> There are a total of 2.3 billion acres in the United States. Urban areas plus highways, nonagricultural roads, railroads, and airports total 61 million acres—just 2.7 percent of the total. Clearly, there is little competition between agriculture and cities and roads... furthermore, between 1.25 million and 1.7 million acres of cropland are being created yearly with irrigation, swamp drainage, and other reclamation techniques. This is a much larger quantity of new farmland than the amount that is converted to cities and highways each year. (Julian L. Simon, "Worldwide, Land for Agriculture is Increasing, Actually," *New York Times*, October 7, 1980, p.23)

Another myth of the antinatalists has it that population growth diminishes the aesthetic qualities of the human condition. Yet some of the world's most beautiful and most livable cities are the most densely settled. Assorted problems, such as traffic congestion and crime, have also been attributed to overpopulation, and with equal lack of evidence. Quite to the contrary, some urban problems become easier to solve as populations grow and become more densely settled. Traffic congestion, for example tends to be more severe in sparsely settled cities like Los Angeles, which rely primarily on personal automobiles for transportation, than in more densely inhabited cities where walking, bicycles, and public transport are common. (Jacequline R. Kasun, "The Love Affair Was a Forced Marriage," *America*, Vol. 129, No. 18.)

But perhaps the main reason why people find it easy to believe in overpopulation is that most of mankind now live, as in ages past, under crowded conditions. Human beings crowd together not because of lack of space on the planet but for one another, to exchange goods and services. Our cities and towns have always thronged with people and traffic—horses, donkeys, and camels in ages past, motor vehicles today. It accounts for the recurring theme throughout history of overpopulation. Plato and Aristotle worried about it half a millennium before Christ; Saint Jerome in the fourth century wrote that, "the world is already full, and the population is too large for the soil." Monasteries, he believed, might solve the problem. None of these earlier city-dwelling philosophers could soar over the earth and see that outside of their immediate view there were almost no people at all.... (Jacqueline R. Kasun, "The War Against Population")

It has been exposed that the entire world population could fit in the state of Texas, each being allotted 2,000 square feet a piece, and the rest of the world would be empty! C.A. Doxiadis and G. Papaioannou, authors of *Ecumenopolis: The Inevitable City of the Future*, estimate that only three-tenths of one percent of the land surface of the earth is used for "human settlements."

Despite a tripling of the world's population in this century, global health and productivity have exploded. Today human beings eat better, produce more, and consume more than ever before in the past... Although some blame dwindling natural resources for the reversals and catastrophes that have recently befallen heavily populated low-income countries, such episodes are directly traceable to the policies or practices of presiding governments. (Nicholas Eberstadt, *The True State of the World*, Chapter 1, R. Bailey, Ed.)

Former Harvard Center for Population Studies Director Roger Revelle estimated that the agricultural resources of the world were capable of providing an adequate diet (2,500 kilocalories per day) for forty billion people, and that it would require the use of less than twenty-five percent of the earth's ice-free land area. Revelle estimated that the less-developed continents were capable of feeding eighteen billion people, and that Africa alone was capable of feeding ten billion people, or twice the current world population, and more than twelve times the 1990 population of Africa.

In his book, *Abortion in the Church*, Max Latham writes the following calculation which he received from Bill Gothard Ministries: "Let's assume that we could place every person in the whole world together shoulder to shoulder in one place on the earth. The current world population is approximately 5 billion people. Let's allow 2.5 square feet of standing room space for each of these 5 billion people.... The total area needed would be 5 billion times 2.5 square feet per person, or 12,500,000,000 square feet. This is equal to approximately 500 square miles. The city limits of Jacksonville, Florida contain

841 square miles. Thus, we could place all the people on earth today in just one city in America and still have plenty of room left over!"

It is the over-population scare that is the problem. It is the mismanagement of resources. King Solomon, who was the wealthiest king who ever lived, reigned over a kingdom that was only 140,000 sq. km (one and a half times the size of Tasmania, Australia), and yet this land supported people who "were many, as the sand which is by the sea in multitude." Did these people live in misery, trying to carve out an existence with limited resources because of over population? No, they lived in good times. Let's read 1 Kings 4:20-34 and see what kind of a life they lived in this limited area, with people swarming like the sand of the sea.

They were prosperous. They had a good life, good times, and plenty to eat. Verse 20 says they were "eating and drinking, and making merry." It doesn't sound like a poverty-stricken land when we read of Solomon's supply for one day: "thirty measures of meal, ten fat oxen, and twenty oxen out of the pastures, and an hundred sheep, beside harts, and roebucks, and fallowdeer, and fatted fowl."

Every family had their own home. "Israel dwelt safely, every man under his vine and under his fig tree...." Read verse 25. There was plenty of work for everyone. Read verses 26-28. There was peace in all the land. Read verse 24.

GREATER POPULATION—
BETTER ECONOMY

A growing population is necessary for a successful economic climate. The Bible links these two factors together. Isaiah 29: 22-23 (TLB) says, "My people will no longer be ashamed. For when they see the surging birth rate and the expanding economy, then they will fear and rejoice in my name."

QUESTIONS

1. If "Be fruitful and multiply" was God's first commandment, why do we often leave it until last? Or ignore it altogether? Can you think of reasons?

_____

_____

_____

2. Why do you think that many Christians today take more notice of the population proponents than they do of what God, who created the earth, says in His Word?

_____

_____

_____

3. According to Isaiah 45:18, why did God create the earth?

_____

_____

_____

4. What are the reasons that stop you from obeying God's first commandment?

_____

_____

_____

CHAPTER 2

*G*OD LOVES INCREASE

God longs for fruitfulness and increase in the natural and in the spiritual sense. He longs for fruitfulness from our marriage unions. When the question is asked in Malachi 2:15, "What does God want from your union?" His answer comes ringing back, "I want a godly seed." This is the desire of God's heart.

When God speaks of blessing, He promises increase of the fruit of the womb, but also of land and the fruit of the ground, of cattle, sheep, and fruitful vineyards. He talks about the increase of wealth, knowledge, and even the increase of the years of our life. God's blessings are enlargement, fruitfulness, and increase.

Look up these Scriptures for further study. They are a few of the many in the Old Testament that reveal God's heart for fruitfulness. God is certainly not silent on this subject: Genesis 1:28; 9:1,7; 16:10; 17:1-6; 18-20; 22:16-17; 24:60; 26:3-4; 28:3;

30:43; 35:11; 47:27; 49:22-26; Exodus 23:26; Leviticus 26:3,9; Deuteronomy 1:10-11; 6:3; 7:13-14; 8:1; 10:22; 13:17; 26:5; 28: 4-11; 30:16; Job 5:25; Psalm 92:12-14; 112:1-2; 115:14; 128:3; Isaiah 54:1-2; 54:1,2; Jeremiah 17:7,8b; 23:3; 29:6; 30:19; 33:22; Ezekiel 36:10-11.

God wanted the children of Israel not only to increase, but to increase *abundantly, exceedingly, mightily, greatly, plenteously, and multitudinously*!

1. Abundantly

Genesis 9:7 says, "And you, be ye fruitful, and multiply; bring forth abundantly in the earth, and multiply therein." The Hebrew word for "abundantly" is *sharats* which means "to swarm or abound." The MLB translation gives a correct rendering when it says, "As for you, be fruitful and multiply, swarm over the earth and multiply it" (Exodus 1:7).

2. Exceedingly

Genesis 16:10 says, "I will multiply thy seed exceedingly, that it shall not be numbered for multitude." The Hebrew word for "exceedingly" is *rabah* which, as we found in chapter one, means "to be many, to be abundant."

The following are other Scriptures where the word *rabah* is used: Genesis 1:28; 9:1,7; 10:10; 17:2,20; 22:17; 26:4,24; 28:3; 35:11; 47:27; Exodus 1:7,12,20; 32:13; Leviticus 26:9; Deuteronomy 1:10; 7:13; 8:1; 13:17; 28:63; 30:5,16; Joshua 24:3; Jeremiah 30:19; 33:22; Ezekiel 16:7; 36:10; 37:26; Hebrews 5:16.

3. Mightily and Greatly

Deuteronomy 6:3, "...that ye may increase mightily, as the Lord God of thy fathers hath promised thee..." Psalm 105:24 says, "He increased his people greatly." The Hebrew word for "mightily" and "greatly" is *meod* which means, "vehemently, whole-heartedly, speedily, diligently." These are very strong words, aren't they? We are to fulfill this commandment with a passion, not reluctantly. Read also 1 Chronicles 4:38 and 107:38.

4. Plenteously

Deuteronomy 30:9, "And the Lord thy God will make thee plenteous in every work of thine hand, in the fruit of thy body..." Read also Deuteronomy 28:11. The word "plenteous" in the Hebrew is *yathar* which means "to jut over or exceed, cause to abound."

5. Multitudinously

Genesis 32:12, "I will surely do thee good, and make thy seed as the sand of the sea, which cannot be numbered for multitude." The Hebrew word for "multitude" is *rob* which is from a root word *rabab* meaning "multiply by the myriad, ten thousands, be increased, more in number."

Leviticus 26:9, "For I will have respect unto you, and make you fruitful, and multiply you..." This Scripture tells us that God shows respect to us by multiplying us.

Deuteronomy 1:10-11, "The Lord your God hath multiplied you, and behold, ye are this day as the stars of heaven for multitude. (The Lord God of your fathers make you a thousand times so many more as ye are, and bless you, as He hath promised you!)"

Proverbs 14:28, "In the multitude of people is the king's honor, but in the want of people is the destruction of the prince."

Other Scriptures where the word *rob* is used: Genesis 16:10; 48:16; Deuteronomy 1:10; 10:22, 28:62; 1 Kings 3:8; 2 Chronicles 1:9.

Exodus 1:7-22 tells us what happened when Israel obeyed God's command to "be fruitful and multiply."

Exodus 1:7 says, "the children of Israel were fruitful, and increased abundantly, and multiplied, and waxed exceeding mighty; and the land was filled with them."

Knox translation says, "the race of Israel grew into a teeming multitude." The implication is that Israel experienced a veritable population explosion.

Deuteronomy 26:5 says, "A Syrian ready to perish was my father, and he went down into Egypt, and sojourned there with a few, and became there a nation, great, mighty, and populous."

What was the outcome of this population explosion?

MORE AND MIGHTIER!

Pharaoh said to the people of Egypt in Exodus 1:9, "the people of the children of Israel are *more and mightier* than we" (emphasis added). Psalm 104:24 tells us that God "increased his people greatly; and *made them stronger than their enemies*" (emphasis added). They were a threat to Egypt. This was God's intention for His covenant people of Israel. And it is still His plan for His people today. He wants His people to become *more and mightier* in the land. He wants the godly seed to be a threat to the devil. Is the Christian church a threat to the devil today? No! Instead, we have given in to the enemy's tactics to deplete the godly seed. There are some Christian couples who voice that they do not want children at all. This is opposite to God's heartbeat and God's Word. If all couples took this attitude, Christianity would be wiped from the earth. It is our children who carry on God's Word from generation to generation. Read Deuteronomy 4:9-10; 6:1-9; Psalm 48:12-14; 78:1-8; 145:5; Isaiah 38:19; 59:21; Jeremiah 32:39; Joel 1:3.

There are many today who have changed the Word of the Lord in Psalm 127:3-4 to their own version, more suited to their lifestyle: "Lo, children are a burden from the Lord: and the fruit of the womb is a curse. Depressed is the man who has children, and happy is the man who avoids them or has as few as possible" (Humanistic Version). How true is the statement of the late Francis Schaeffer, "Tell me what the world is saying today, and I'll tell you what the church will be saying seven years from now."

One of the biggest threats to the devil is husbands and wives who understand God's revelation for marriage and who will bring forth godly offspring for His glory. The devil is frightened of the godly seed, for it is they who will destroy his works in this world.

The enemy knew that God would need an army in this hour to fulfill His great purposes. He knew that if he could diminish God's army, he could thwart God's plans. It is the strategy of Satan to minimize the holy seed. The sad thing is that the Christian church has unconsciously fallen into this trap. As Christians in the last few decades have decided to have fewer children, they have limited the power of God on earth. God's plan is to fill the earth with His glory. God calls the increase of children our "glory" (Hosea 9:11).

Instead of becoming *more and mightier*, we are becoming less and less. Christians are having as few children as the world. Instead of obeying the Word of God, we have followed the trends of the world. There was a time when Christians believed God and equated children with blessings. But the world, which did not know God, found children a nuisance and hindrance to their lifestyle, so they began to limit their family to two children or perhaps no children at all. Was this God's heartbeat? No! But the church, which is "the pillar and ground of truth," looked on and thought, "What a great idea. I think we will follow the world. We will be able to accomplish a lot more in life without the encumbrance of children." And so the church forgot God's plan for mankind and gradually succumbed to this humanistic trend.

With the availability of better and safer methods of contraception, worldly couples were able to delay childbearing until they purchased their home, accumulated their material possessions, and felt they were ready to start a family. Is this trend grounded in the Scriptures? No! But once again,

Christian couples looked at the world and thought, "What a great idea. The world sure knows best. The Bible is archaic. We will go the world's way." And so now it is considered normal in the Christian church for couples to wait a few years before they have a family.

PREPARE FOR FRUITFULNESS

It is important that a husband-to-be work hard to prepare himself before marriage so that he is in a position to provide for his wife and family. It is the task of parents to teach their sons that they cannot fritter away their means, but that they have a responsibility to work hard, save, and prepare themselves to support a wife and family.

We should teach our sons as they grow up that God has placed the responsibility upon them to one day provide for a family. They should know the Scripture in 1 Timothy 5:8, "But if any provide not for his own, and especially for those of his own house, he hath denied the faith, and is worse than an infidel." If a young man cannot support a wife and family, he is not yet ready for marriage. It is an indictment against the training of our children if our sons grow up unprepared for this task. It is sad to hear so many young Christian wives share that their husbands do not want them to have any more children because they want them to go out to work to help support the home. This is not biblical and maligns the Word of God.

THE FIRST BLESSING

Deuteronomy 28 is a special portion of the Word of God. It tells us all the blessings that will come upon us if we walk according to God's commandments. Once again, God puts first things first. Before He promises the blessings of the fruit of the ground, the increase of livestock, and a prosperous business, He says in verse 11 that He first blesses the fruit of the womb. This is the highest blessing that God gives.

God is a God of increase. He wants His kingdom to increase on earth. He wants to fill His eternal kingdom. Isaiah 9:7 says, "Of the increase of His government and peace there shall be no end." The Living Bible calls it "His *ever-expanding* government" (emphasis added).

Remember how God likens His kingdom to a little mustard seed? It is one of the smallest seeds, but grows to be one of the largest of trees. Mark 4:30-32 says, "Whereunto shall we liken the kingdom of God? or with what comparison shall we compare it? It is like a grain of mustard seed, which, when it is sown in the earth, is less than all the seeds that be in the earth: But when it is sown, it grows up, and becomes greater than all herbs, and shoots out great branches; so that the fowls of the air may lodge under the shadow of it."

God has put this same desire for enlargement and increase within us. A businessman naturally wants to expand his business. A farmer wants more land, more cattle, or more sheep. A pastor wants his church to grow. We desire more knowledge. We desire to increase our wealth. We would like to live in a bigger home. We naturally desire enlargement, increase, and fruitfulness.

Hosea 10:1 is an interesting Scripture: "Israel is an empty vine, he bringeth forth fruit unto himself." If we bring forth fruit unto ourselves and reject fruitfulness for the sake of fulfilling our own desires and pursuits, it will only produce emptiness. A vine that is empty and bears no fruit is useless. A fruitful vine gives blessing to many. What does God call the wife? A "fruitful vine." The Hebrew translation is literally a "prolific vine" (Psalm 128:3).

LIKE A FLOCK

Psalm 107:38,41 (NEB) says, "He blesses them and their numbers increase... and makes families increase like flocks of sheep." One or two sheep is not a flock. God wants our families to be like a flock. The family is where God loves people to be nurtured. His desire is for children to be in an environment with brothers and sisters, like a flock. When the Word says, "God sets the solitary in families," in Psalm 68:6, it means that He puts the "forsaken" and "lonely" in a family, but it also means that He will bless an "only child" by giving them family. The Hebrew word for "solitary" is *yachid* which means "an only child."

We receive the same understanding from Psalm 128:3 where God reveals to us a picture of a family that is blessed of the Lord. As we peek through the window to get a glimpse of what this family is like, we see all the children sitting around the family table: "Thy wife shall be as a fruitful vine by the sides of thine house: thy children like olive plants round about thy table." The Living Bible amplifies this passage, "Look at all those children! There they sit around the dinner table as vigorous and healthy as young olive trees." It is difficult for one or two children to encompass the whole dinner table. God wants every chair around the table to be filled.

WITHOUT NUMBER

When God talks about blessing families with fruitfulness, He likens it to things that cannot be numbered. This is the bigness of His vision. Look up these amazing Scriptures:

1. The stars of the heavens. Look up: Genesis 15:5; 22:17; 26:4; Exodus 32:13; Deuteronomy 1:10; 10:22; 28:62; 1 Chronicles 27:23b; Nehemiah 9:23; Jeremiah 33:22; Hebrews 11:12.

2. The dust of the earth. Look up: Genesis 13:16; 28:14; Numbers 23:10; 2 Chronicles 1:9.

3. The sands of the seashore. Look up: Genesis 22:17; 32:12; Isaiah 48:18,19; Jeremiah 33:22; Hosea 1:10; Hebrews 11: 12.

4. The grass of the fields. Look up Job 5:25. And the "bud of the field." Ezekiel 16:7.

5. Thousands of millions that speak of that which cannot be numbered. The blessing over Rebekah in preparation for her marriage to Isaac was, "Be thou the mother of thousands of millions…" Look up: Genesis 24:60.

IN DIFFICULT TIMES, TOO

The children of Israel did not obey God's commandment "to be fruitful and multiply" just when it suited them, or only in good economic times. No, they obeyed, no matter what the circumstances.

During Slavery:

They obeyed when they were in slavery in Egypt. They multiplied in the face of persecution. Exodus 1:11-12 (TJB) tells the story, "They put slave drivers over the Israelites to wear them down under heavy loads… But the more they were crushed, the more they increased and spread…" Our mentality is that if we are going through persecution, difficult times, or money is tight, that we cannot have children. The Israelites proved that God was able to keep them and provide for them, even in the most difficult times, times of "affliction" and "bitter with hard bondage." None of us have had to face the persecution and trials that they faced at that time, but they still kept multiplying.

During Captivity:

Even when God pronounced judgment on Judah and sent them into captivity as slaves of Babylon, He did not release them from His command to multiply. He told them through Jeremiah the prophet in Jeremiah 29:5-6, "Thus saith the Lord of hosts, the God of Israel, unto all that are carried away captives... Take ye wives and beget sons and daughters; and take wives for your sons, and give your daughters to husbands, that they may bear sons and daughters; that ye may be increased there, and not diminished."

Yes, Even in the City:

Deuteronomy 28:2-4, "Blessed shalt thou be in the city, and blessed shalt thou be in the field. Blessed shall be the fruit of thy body..." Sometimes we hear folks saying that it is too hard to have children when living in the city. It is okay for those who live in the country, but what about us who are squashed up in the city? God promises that He will bless us in the city as well as the country, immediately before He says that He will bless the fruit of our womb. Isn't that wonderful?

GOD IS GLORIFIED BY INCREASE

Isaiah 26:15, "Thou hast increased the nation, O Lord, Thou hast increased the nation... Thou art glorified." Jeremiah 30: 19, "I will multiply them, and they shall not be few; I will also glorify them, and they shall not be small." The way that God honored Israel was by multiplying them!

BARRENNESS IS A CURSE

In the Word of God, fruitfulness of the womb is always considered a blessing. Barrenness was considered a curse, a shame and a disgrace. God's blessing on His people was multiplication. When they sinned and He had to bring judgment, it was usually by thinning their numbers. Look up these verses: Deuteronomy 4:27; 28:18; Hosea 4:10; 9:11-17.

Leviticus 26:21-22, "If ye walk contrary unto Me, and will not hearken unto Me; I will bring seven times more plagues upon you according to your sins. I will also send wild beasts among you, which shall rob you of your children, and destroy your cattle, and make you few in number..."

Deuteronomy 28:62, "You shall be left few in number, whereas you were as the stars of heaven in multitude, because you would not obey the voice of the Lord your God."

Psalm 106:14-15 (AMP), God "sent leanness into their soul and thinned their numbers by disease and death." This was also God's judgment on Israel.

Ezekiel 19:10-14 is an allegory about Israel where she is likened to a mother. As we read this portion of Scripture, we catch sight of a picture of motherhood as God sees it, and then as it has degenerated today. God says that motherhood is exalted above everything else, but the enemy has sought to destroy this God-given career. God personifies mothers with fruitfulness. She is meant to be "fruitful and full of branches." But when the glory of motherhood is cast down, the fruitfulness disappears. This Scripture says her fruit (the children from her womb) is "dried up" (v.12) and it is "devoured" (v.14). We see this happening today. Many mothers are voluntarily causing their wombs to be "dried up." Others are too late for childbearing. When they eventually decide to have a child, they are no longer fertile. The fruit of the womb is "devoured" from others by drugs, abortions, and early hysterectomies. Is this a matter for rejoicing? No! This passage ends with a funeral dirge, "This is a lamentation and shall be for a lamentation!"

Hosea 9:11-16 is also a sad passage. The "glory" of Ephraim was their "fruitfulness" which was the prophetic word given over them. Read Genesis 49:22-26 and Deuteronomy 33:13-17. Even the name of Ephraim means "double fruitfulness." It is a dual form of *Ephrath* which means "fruitfulness." But in this passage, God judges Ephraim for their sin and turning away from His ways. God's judgment was to take away their "glory" which was their children by "miscarrying wombs and dry breasts."

Hosea 9:11, "Ephraim's glory shall fly away like a bird—no birth, no pregnancy, no conception!" This was God's judgment on Ephraim.

In Luke 1:24-25, Elizabeth said, "He looked with favor upon me to take away my disgrace among women." Barrenness was considered a disgrace. Isn't it incredible that today many women choose disgrace?

DON'T LEAVE IT TOO LATE

We cannot take our fertility for granted. It is a very precious gift that we cannot trifle with. We cannot decide ourselves when we want a child. Fertility is ultimately in the hands of God, and He tells us in His Word the best time for bringing forth children—when we are young. I was talking to a woman in her thirties the other evening who shared with me how she had been deceived. She said, "I was encouraged to pursue my career at the expense of children. Now I am desperate to have children and have been trying for over a year but still have not conceived." Has she waited too long? This testimony can be repeated over and over again. Psalm 127:4 says, "As arrows are in the hand of a mighty man; so are children of the *youth*" (emphasis added).

Further passages: Proverbs 2:17; 5:18; Isaiah 54:6; Joel 1: 8; Malachi 2:15.

An *Above Rubies* reader wrote to me recently and shared, "I am a registered nurse, and many older people whom I've cared for are now in their eighties and nineties and were having their families during The Depression. They were a generation who tried hard to limit their family size. I've held so many old, frail hands and listened to so many sweet souls tell me how they regretted not having more children. It is such a common thread and it is so typical of our enemy. First he tricks people into not letting God bless them with a big family, then when they are old, he torments them with their error."

NEW TESTAMENT SCRIPTURES FRUIT, MORE FRUIT, MUCH FRUIT

What about the New Testament? Just as God desires fruitfulness in the natural, He also desires fruitfulness in our spiritual lives. He has chosen us to be spiritually fruitful, too. He looks for fruit. John 15:16 says, "I have chosen you and ordained you that you should go and bring forth *fruit…*" (emphasis added). As we continue to read John 15, we see that God is not satisfied with average fruitfulness. He says He wants us to bring forth "more fruit" in verse 2. Still that is not enough, and in verse 8, He says, "Herein is my Father glorified, that ye bear *much fruit*; so shall ye be my disciples" (emphasis added).

The more fruit that we bring forth, the more we glorify the Father. Fruitfulness is what satisfies His heart. In fact, in verse 2, He says strong words, "Every branch in Me that beareth not fruit, He taketh away." This is God's desire for the natural and the spiritual. 1 Corinthians 15:46 tells us that the natural comes first and then the spiritual.

BORN TO BE FRUIT BEARERS

This is God's desire for us, naturally and spiritually. The Message Bible translation of John 15:16 says, "You did not choose me, remember; I chose you, and put you in the world to bear fruit,

fruit that won't spoil. As *fruit bearers*, whatever you ask the Father in relation to me, he gives you" (emphasis added).

We know that one of the greatest reasons for marriage is to show forth the picture of Christ and His church. It is also the desire of Christ that His body is fruitful. When we are fruitful in our marriage, we are revealing a true picture of Christ and the church to the world.

WE WERE BORN TO REPRODUCE!

All nature and all mankind were created for this purpose. This is God's plan for us in the natural and in the spiritual.

JESUS LIVED IN A BIG FAMILY

Mark 6:3 tells us, "Is not this the carpenter, the son of Mary, the brother of James, and Joses, and of Juda and Simon? And are not his sisters here with us?" There would have been a minimum of seven children in Joseph and Mary's family. The names of five sons are mentioned and the sisters are stated in plural, which would be a minimum of two, but there could have been five daughters as well, or even more. Maybe there were ten children in the family! God wanted His son to enjoy the blessing of being part of large family.

JESUS LOVES THE CHILDREN

Jesus always welcomed the children. When the disciples tried to send them away, He rebuked them and drew the children to Him.

Matthew 19:14 (MLB), "But Jesus said, 'Allow the little ones and do not stop them from coming to Me, for of this kind the kingdom of heaven is composed.'"

Matthew 19:14 (Williams), "Let the little children alone, and stop preventing them from coming to Me." It took a long time for the disciples to receive Jesus' message about children. Jesus had just spoken to them about embracing children in the previous chapter and yet they are still pushing the children away! How sad it is that those who confess Jesus is their Lord do not have the same heart that He has about children. Instead, they do everything in their power to stop the children coming.

THE GOD OF THE FULL HOUSE

Luke 14:23, "Go out into the highways and hedges, and compel them to come in, that my house may be filled." God is the God of the full house. He wants to fill eternity. He will embrace all who will come to Him in His family. Do we have the same heart that God has? Do we want to fill our homes with furniture, televisions, and material possessions—or children? Are our homes filled with lasting treasures? The current statistics in the United States reveal that there are more televisions per households than there are children! What an indictment against a nation!

Theodore Laetsch states, "The two-children system will rapidly lead to extermination of a people, for ten per-cent of all marriages are naturally childless, and unmarried people do not contribute to the growth of a nation, while the two-children system replaces only the parents, no replacements for unmarried people and childless couples, hence a decrease in population, and the nation will die out. At least four children to a family to prevent this dying out, five children to bring about an increase in population."

God has a big heart. He wants a big family. If God is truly dwelling in our hearts, we will think like He thinks. This will also be our vision.

QUESTIONS

1. Give reasons why we want increase in every aspect of our lives, except children? What has caused this mentality?

   _____

   _____

   _____

2. Read Psalm 128:3. What kind of wife is in the home that God desires to bless? How can she fulfill this description?

   _____

   _____

   _____

3. When did the children of Israel become a threat to Pharaoh and the people of Egypt? How does this relate to the church today?

   _____

   _____

   _____

4. In Jeremiah 50:11, God calls Babylon, "the destroyers of my heritage." Who are the destroyers of God's heritage today?

_____

_____

_____

5. What are the four metaphors God uses to describe the blessing of fruitfulness in families?

a. Genesis 15:5

_____

b. Genesis 13:16

_____

c. Genesis 22:17

_____

d. Job 5:25

_____

6. In light of the above Scriptures, in what ways do I need to get my attitude in line with God's attitude about children?

_____

_____

_____

7. a. When do you think parents should start training their sons for fatherhood and how to provide for their families?

_____

_____

_____

b. State ways you think this teaching can be accomplished effectively, so our young men will grow up, ready to face the responsibilities of fatherhood and provision.

_____

_____

_____

CHAPTER 3

𝒯HE BLESSING

God's Blessing on Marriage is the Blessing of Children

Read Genesis 1:28 again and you will notice that God blesses Adam and Eve before He commands them to be fruitful and multiply. Fruitfulness is God's blessing. It is the first and highest blessing that God gives to marriage. In fact, we cannot receive fruitfulness without God first blessing us. We see this truth reiterated throughout the Word. Take time to read these Scriptures (emphasis added).

Genesis 9:1,2,7, "And God *blessed* Noah and his sons, and said unto them, be fruitful and multiply, and replenish the earth."

Genesis 17:15-17, "And God said unto Abraham, As for Sarai thy wife, thou shalt not call her name Sarai, but Sarah shall her name be. And I will *bless* her, and give thee a son also of her: yes, I will *bless* her, and she shall be a mother of nations; kings of people shall be of her."

Genesis 17:20, "As for Ishmael, Behold, I have *blessed* him, and will make him fruitful, and will multiply him exceedingly...."

Genesis 22:17-18, "In *blessing* I will *bless* thee, and in multiplying I will multiply thy seed as the stars of the heaven, and as the sand which is upon the seashore… and in thy seed shall all the nations of the earth be blessed; because thou hast obeyed my voice."

Genesis 24:60, "They *blessed* Rebekah, and said unto her, be thou the mother of thousands of millions."

Genesis 28:1-3, "God Almighty *bless* thee, and make thee fruitful, and multiply thee, that thou mayest be a multitude of people."

Genesis 30:13, "Happy am I for the daughters will call me *blessed* and she called his name Asher." ("Asher" and "blessed" both mean "happiness.")

Genesis 48:3,4, "And Jacob said… God Almighty appeared unto me and *blessed* me… and said unto me, Behold I will make thee fruitful and multiply thee, and I will make of thee a multitude of people.…"

Genesis 49:25, "By the God of thy father, who shall help thee; and by the Almighty, who shall *bless* thee with… *blessings* of the breasts, and of the womb."

Leviticus 26:3,9, "If ye walk in my statues and keep my commandments and do them… *I will have respect unto you, and make you fruitful, and multiply you.*"

Deuteronomy 1:10-11, "The Lord your God hath multiplied you, and behold, ye are this day as the stars of heaven for multitude. The Lord God of your fathers make you a *thousand times so many more as ye are, and bless you, as he hath promised you!"* Abraham is blessing the Israelites with God's blessing. Do you feel God's heart beating with Abraham's heart as he speaks these words? Abraham also understood that it is only God who can give the blessing of conception and fruitfulness. He says, "The Lord make you…" It is the blessing of God.

Deuteronomy 7:12-16, "Wherefore it shall come to pass, if ye hearken to these judgments, and keep, and do them, that… He will love thee, and *bless* thee, and multiply thee: He will also *bless* the fruit of thy womb…. Thou shalt be *blessed* above all people: *there shall not be male or female barren among you…"*

Deuteronomy 13:17, "…that the Lord may turn from the fierceness of His anger and *show you mercy, have compassion on you and multiply* you, just as He swore to your fathers."

Deuteronomy 28:1-10, "If thou shalt hearken diligently unto the voice of the Lord thy God, to observe and to do all His commandments which I command thee this day, that… all these *blessings* shall come on thee, and overtake thee…. *Blessed* shall be the fruit of thy womb…."

Deuteronomy 33:24, "And of Asher he said, Let Asher be *blessed* with children."

Deuteronomy 28:63, "…the Lord *rejoiced over you to do you good*, and to multiply you."

Deuteronomy 30:5, "He will *do thee good*, and multiply thee above thy fathers."

1 Chronicles 26:4-5, "The sons of Obededom were, Shemaiah the firstborn, Jehozabad the second, Joah the

third, Sacar the fourth, Nethaneel the fifth, Ammiel the sixth, Issachar the seventh, Peulthai the eighth: *for God blessed him!*" The Living Bible says, "What a blessing God gave him with all those sons!"

Job 42:12-15, "So the Lord *blessed* the latter end of Job more than his beginning…. he had seven sons and three daughters."

Psalm 107:38, "He *blesses* them also, so that they are multiplied greatly."

Psalm 115:12-15, "The Lord hath been mindful of us: He will *bless* us… The Lord shall increase you more and more, you and your children. Ye are *blessed* of the Lord which made heaven and earth."

Psalm 127:3-5, "Lo, children are an heritage of the Lord: and the fruit of the womb is His reward. As arrows are in the hand of a mighty man; so are children of the youth. *Happy* is the man that hath his quiver full of them: they shall not be ashamed but they shall speak with the enemies in the gate." GNB translation says, "Children are a gift from the Lord; they are a real *blessing.*"

Psalm 128, "*Blessed* is every one that feareth the Lord: that walketh in His ways…. *Happy* shalt thou be, and it shall be well with thee. Thy wife shall be as a fruitful vine ["within your house" (NAS)]: thy children like olive plants round about thy table. Behold that thus shall the man be *blessed* that feareth the Lord." This Scripture reveals a picture of a man that is blessed of the Lord. It doesn't say that he has great possessions, houses, and land or that he has made it to the top in his career. No, the hallmark of the man who is blessed of the Lord is the one who is blessed with well-behaved children. This is the true mark of success.

Isaiah 51:2, "Look unto Abraham your father, and unto Sarah that bare you; for I called him alone, and *blessed* him and increased him."

Jeremiah 30:19 (GNB), "By *my blessing* they will increase in numbers."

Luke 1:28,31, "And the angel came in unto her, and said, Hail... *blessed* art thou among women.... behold, thou shalt conceive in thy womb, and bring forth a son, and shalt call His name Jesus."

We see from the above Scriptures that conception is a result of God's blessing upon our lives. We also see that when God wanted to bless a couple, He blessed them with children. When God says, "I want to bless you," our response is often "Thank you, Lord.... I need a new car.... I need a new house.... that will be great." But God says, "Just a minute, I want to bless you with a little baby... I want a godly offspring." At this point, many decide they don't want God's blessings!

GOD'S NUMBER ONE BLESSING IS MULTIPLICATION

What was the greatest blessing God promised His people when they would return to Israel from their captive lands? It was the blessing of multiplication. God's blessing is not zero-population, but maximum population.

Isaiah 49:19-20, "the land shall be too narrow by reason of the inhabitants."

Jeremiah 31:27 (TLB), "The time will come when I will greatly increase the population."

Jeremiah 33:21, "As the host of heaven cannot be numbered, neither the sand of the sea measured: so will I multiply the seed of David my servant, and the Levites that minister unto me."

Ezekiel 36:10 (MLB), "I will multiply you into a large population."

Ezekiel 36:37-38, "I will increase them with men like a flock.... so shall the waste cities be filled with flocks of men: and they shall know that I am the Lord."

Zechariah 2:4, "Jerusalem shall be inhabited as towns without walls for the multitude of men and cattle therein."

Zechariah 10:8-10, "I will bring them again.... and gather them... and I will bring them into the land of Gilead and Lebanon; and a place shall not be found for them."

BLESSED ABOVE ALL PEOPLE

In Deuteronomy 7:14, God says, "Thou shalt be *blessed above all people.*"

What was the blessing that set the children of Israel apart from all other people? Let's read it straight from the Bible: "There shall not be male or female barren among you...." It was the blessing of fruitfulness.

QUESTIONS

1. What picture does the Word of God paint of a godly man? Read Psalm 128 again.

   _____

   _____

   _____

2. The Scriptures we have read reveal that children are the result of the blessing of God. If this is so, why do you think so many couples do not want to receive God's blessings?

   _____

   _____

   _____

3. Some like to receive a few blessings but then take action
    for God to stop further "blessings." How does this line up
    with God's Word?

    _____

    _____

    _____

4. Read Hosea 9:11. What does God call our children?

    _____

    _____

    _____

CHAPTER 4

GIFTS FROM GOD

Children Are God's Gift to Marriage

The following Scriptures reveal that children are God's gifts to us. They are gifts from His bountiful hand. The mother of the very first child who was born acknowledges him as a gift from the Lord.

Genesis 4:1, "And Adam knew Eve his wife; and she conceived and bare Cain, and said, *I have gotten a man from the Lord.*"

Jacob acknowledged this truth: Genesis 33:5, "And he lifted up his eyes, and saw the women and the children; and said, Who are those with thee? And he said, The children which *God hath graciously given* thy servant."

Joseph acknowledged this truth: Genesis 48:9, "They are my sons, whom *God hath given me* in this place."

Joshua acknowledged this truth: Joshua 24:3, "I took your father Abraham… and multiplied his seed, and *gave him Isaac.*"

David and the Psalmists acknowledged this truth: 1 Chronicles 28:5 (NAS), David said, "*The Lord has given me many sons.*"

Psalm 127:3-5 (NEB), "Sons are a *gift* from the Lord and children a reward from him. Like arrows in the hand of a fighting man are the sons of a man's youth. Happy is the man who has his quiver full of them; such men shall not be put to shame when they confront their enemies in court."

Psalm 127:3 (KNOX), "Fatherhood itself is the *Lord's gift*, the fruitful womb is a reward that *comes from him.*"

Martin Luther comments on this verse, "Genesis 9:1 leads us to believe that children are a gift of God and come solely through the blessing of God, just as Psalm 127:3 shows. The heathen, who have not been instructed by the Word of God, believe that the propagation of the human race happens partly by nature, partly by accident, especially since those who are regarded as most suited for procreation often fail to have children. Therefore the heathen do not thank God for this gift, nor do they receive their children as the gift of God."

Other biblical writers revealed this truth also:

Ruth 4:13b, "The *Lord gave her conception*, and she bare a son."

1 Chronicles 25:4-6, "Bukkiah, Mattaniah, Uzziel, Shebuel, and Jerimoth, Hannaniah, Hanani, Eliathah, Giddalti, and Romamti-ezer, Joshbekashah, Mallothi, Hothir, and Mahazioth: all these were the sons of Heman the king's seer in the words of God, to lift up the horn. And *God gave to Heman* fourteen sons and three daughters. All these were under the

hands of their father for song in the house of the Lord, with cymbals, psalteries, and harps, for the service of the house of God, according to the king's order..."

Isaiah 8:18, "Behold, I and the *children whom the Lord hath given me* are for signs and for wonders in Israel *from the Lord of hosts*, which dwells in mount Zion."

GOD SAYS CHILDREN ARE HIS BEST GIFT!

The Message Bible translation of Psalm 127:3 says, "Don't you see that children are God's *best* gift? the fruit of the womb His generous legacy?"

The Moffat's translation says, "Sons are a gift from the eternal and children are a *boon* from Him."

HOW SHOULD WE RECEIVE A GIFT?

We see from the above Scriptures that children are a gift from God. What should we do with a gift, especially a gift from God? Reject it or receive it? How should we receive the gift of children?

Matthew 18:5 says, "Whoso shall receive one such little child in my name receiveth Me."

The word "receive" that is used here is the Greek word *dechomal* which means to "accept a gift deliberately and readily; to receive heartily; reaching out eagerly to receive something; looking for; waiting with earnest expectation."

Check also Luke 9:48. It is different from when the word *lambano* is used which means to receive without necessarily a favorable reception. Matthew 18:5 tells us that when we receive a little child, we are actually receiving Jesus Himself. To welcome a baby is to welcome Jesus! Should we receive Jesus with a half-hearted attitude? Some folks are adamant that they don't want to have children at all. Others will say, "Well, if God gives us one, we will accept, but we're not trying." This Scripture says that we are to intentionally desire the gift of children, to reach out eagerly to receive them.

Jesus expands this truth further in John 13:20, "Verily, verily, I say unto you, He that receiveth whomsoever I send receiveth me; and he that receiveth me receiveth Him that sent me." Are we willing to readily and whole-heartedly receive any child that God would give to us, and as many as He has planned to give to us? What if we don't want them, because we are too busy with other plans? This Scripture plainly tells us that when we refuse the children whom God would send, we are actually refusing Jesus Himself.

We see a glimpse of God's heart toward babies in 2 Samuel 12:2, "And David comforted Bathsheba his wife, and went in unto her, and lay with her, and she bare a son, and he called his name Solomon; and the Lord loved him."

"And the Lord loved him"—this little phrase speaks a thousand words. God loves babies. He delights in every new child who is born into this world.

We see a glimpse of Jesus' heart in Matthew 19:14 which we repeat again, "Suffer the little children, and forbid them not, to come unto Me: for of such is the kingdom of heaven." Jesus' attitude toward children is "Come to Me." What is our attitude?

Matthew 25:40, "Inasmuch as ye have done it unto one of the least of these my brethren, ye have done it unto me." Does this Scripture touch your heart like it does mine? God sees our attitude toward receiving children as our attitude and response to Him! What a challenge.

CONCEPTION IS A VISITATION FROM GOD

Would you like a visit from God? Wow, what an awesome thought! Look at the following Scriptures that tell us that God visited these women to give them conception.

Genesis 21:1, "And the Lord visited Sarah as He had said and the Lord did unto Sarah as He had spoken. For Sarah conceived and bare Abraham a son in his old age."

1 Samuel 2:20-21, "And the Lord visited Hannah so that she conceived and bare three sons and two daughters." And this was after she had given birth to Samuel.

Yes, when you conceived a baby or will conceive a baby in the future, God Almighty visits you! He is the one who gives conception!

WHY DOES GOD GIVE US CHILDREN?

1. To Procreate the Earth

To procreate the earth as we have already discussed. Genesis 1:28.

2. To Honor Us

Talking about Heman in 1 Chronicles 25:4-6, The Living Bible says, "God honored him with fourteen sons and three daughters." The Berkeley, NIV, GNB, RSV, and AMPLIFED versions say that God "exalted" him and gave him more "power" by giving him seventeen children. The NEB says his children were, "given to him through the promises of God for his greater glory." God did not give Heman children to degrade him, as some would think today, but to exalt him. God gives us children to bless us, honor us, and give us greater glory and power in the earth. The more godly children we have, the more power we have for God in the earth. The more "arrows" we raise for God, the more power we have over the enemy, and the more honor we receive and the more glory God receives. Read Jeremiah 30:19.

It is noteworthy that God commences the blessing chapter of Deuteronomy 28 with these words, "God will set thee on high above all nations of the earth." He then proceeds to say how He will do this—by pouring out abundant blessings, the greatest being the blessing of the fruit of the womb. God's Word says that the blessing of children will set us on high, not bring us low. It will cause us to be "the head, and not the tail." We will be "above and not beneath."

The world looks upon those who have a large family to be inferior. This is the deception of the enemy, the one who is called the Deceiver and the Liar. This thinking is opposite to the truth of the Word of God that says that the blessing of family will set us on high.

Check these Scriptures also: Exodus 20:12; Deuteronomy 5:16; Psalm 107:41; Matthew 15:4; Ephesians 6:2-3.

3. To Do Us Good

When God wants to do something good for us, He gives us children. When God rejoices over us, He multiplies us. In the following verses, the word "good" or the phrase "be well with thee" is the word *yatav*. It means, "to be good, to make well, to be beautiful, to be pleasant, to be lovely, to be sound, happy, successful, to make better, to be glad and cheerful." God is in covenant relationship with His people and therefore He blesses them.

Genesis 32:12, "I will surely do thee good, and make thy seed as the sand of the sea…"

BE FRUITFUL AND MULTIPLY

Deuteronomy 6:3, "Hear therefore, O Israel, and observe to do it, that it may be well with thee, and that ye may increase mightily."

Deuteronomy 7:13, "He will love thee, and bless thee, and multiply thee: He will also bless the fruit of thy womb."

Deuteronomy 13:17, "That the Lord may... shew thee mercy, and have compassion upon thee, and multiply thee...." This blessing comes after the people have fulfilled judgment on all those who turn away to worship false gods.

Deuteronomy 28:11a (NIV, RSV), "The Lord will grant you abundant prosperity, in the fruit of your womb..."

Deuteronomy 28:63a, "...the Lord rejoiced over you to do you good, and to multiply you..."

Deuteronomy 30:5, "He will do thee good, and multiply thee..."

Deuteronomy 30:9, "And the Lord thy God will make thee plenteous in every work of thine hand, in the fruit of thy body... for good: for the Lord will again rejoice over thee for good, as he rejoiced over thy fathers."

Deuteronomy 30:15-16, "I have set before thee this day life and good... keep His commandment and His statutes and His judgments, that thou mayest live and multiply: and the Lord thy God shall bless thee..."

Psalm 115:12-15 (RSV), "May the Lord give you increase, you and your children! May you be blessed by the Lord who made heaven and earth!"

4. To Give Us Joy and Delight

Luke 1:13-17 (TJB) says, "Your wife Elizabeth is to bear you a son... he will be your joy and delight ... and many will rejoice at his birth." In this Scripture, God gives two reasons for giving baby John to Zechariah and Elizabeth. First, He says that he will give them *joy and delight*. God gives us children to bring us great joy, gladness, and happiness. Would you like to have more joy and happiness? Then receive the gifts God wants to give you. Psalm 127:5 says, "*Happy* is the man who has his quiver full of children." It doesn't say he'll be ashamed. It doesn't say he'll be miserable. It says he will be *happy*! Does God lie?

Godly children bring much joy to a marriage. The older you get and the more you mature, the more you realize that every other "thing" we strive after in this life is fleeting and will pass away. It is only our children that are lasting gifts that we will keep forever. We can take them into eternity with us. Everything else will be left behind. Wise couples will want the gifts that are lasting.

In Ezekiel 24:25 (Jerusalem Bible), we read what God thinks of our children, "And son of man, on the very day I deprive them of their sons and daughters who are their... strength, their pride and glory, the delight of their eyes, the joy of their hearts..."

In Hosea 9:16, God doesn't just call our children the "fruit of the womb", but the "beloved fruit of the womb." Look at some other translations:

NIV	"cherished offspring"
RV	"beloved children"
NAS	"precious ones"
NEB	"dearest offspring"
JER	"darlings"
NAS	"treasures of the womb"

Now there are some good names to call your little "lambs."

5. For the Service of God

Luke 1:15-17 tells us that John was not only given to Zechariah and Elizabeth to give them great joy but for a specific purpose: "He will bring many of the sons of Israel to the Lord their God... to turn the hearts of fathers toward their children and the disobedient back to the wisdom of the just, preparing for the Lord a people fit for Him." Every child that God gives to us comes into the world with a destiny planned by God.

We read in 1 Chronicles 25 that Heman's children gave him more power and blessing. But ultimately these children were given to him to help him in his service for God. "They were all under the direction of their father to sing in the temple of the Lord, for the service of God's temple with cymbals, harps, and lyres." Our children are given to us to train for the service of God. They are given to us to prepare for the specific purpose that God has planned for them.

In Amos 2:11, God says, "I raised up some of your sons for prophets, and some of your young men for Nazarites." God has a purpose for every child.

6.   A Gift to the Nations

Jeremiah 1:5 says, "Before I formed thee in the womb I knew thee; and before thou camest forth out of the womb I sanctified thee, and I ordained thee a prophet unto the nations." As I checked the word "ordained" in my concordance, I was amazed to notice that the Hebrew word *nathan* is a primary root word meaning "to give." God planned Jeremiah's future before he was even conceived! And God gave him as a "gift" to the nations.

Every child is a gift to the world! Isn't that exciting? Our children are not only a gift from God to us, but also a gift to others. Each child God has given you is a gift from God to the world. Who knows which one will be another David, or Paul, or Einstein, or Billy Graham! Or anointed and faithful builders, teachers, store managers, or whatever! And of course, godly mothers and fathers. Praise God, the world will never be the same because of the children that you have brought into the world and will bring into the world.

7.   To Defend Us and Protect Us

Psalm 127:5 tells us that the man who has his quiver full of arrows will never be defeated when he meets his enemies in the place of judgment. He will have children who will stand up for him and fight for him.

8.   To Help Us

Jeremiah 10:20 tells the plight of the man whose children are all gone and he now has no one to help him set up his tent.

"My tabernacle is spoiled, and all my cords are broken: my children are gone forth of me, and they are not: there is none to stretch forth my tent any more, and to set up my curtains." The more children we have, the more help we have around the home. (Now that all of our children have left home and married, I have to do all the dishes and chores myself!)

Many larger families experience the truth of this Scripture. As they train their children in a good work ethic and the running of the home, the mother of the home has less and less to do. Many young mothers stop having children after two or three because they are so overwhelmed with the busyness of caring for their little ones. It is true that this is the busiest time of motherhood. Your children are all little and are not yet at an age where they can help and pull their weight. But look to the future. These little ones will grow older and as they do they become wonderful helpers. There is a mother in our community of Hickman County who was blessed with nineteen children. Nine of her children are now grown and have left home but there are still ten children at home. She trained them well and confesses that she now lives "like a Queen." By the way, before you start imagining a worn-out old lady after having nineteen children, this mother is fit, in-shape, vibrant and beautiful. It's hard to believe she has had even two children!

9. To Care for Us When We Are Older

Read Proverbs 23:22; Matthew 15:4-8; Mark 7:9-13; John 19:25-27; 1 Timothy 5:3,4,8,16. As you can see, there are many

Scriptures about this subject. God's plan is that the younger generation will care for the older generation. This also affects the whole nation. If we do not have the children God has destined for us to have, there will be an imbalance in the population— there will be more older people than younger people.

10. For God Himself

This is the highest reason. Although God gives us the joy of children for the above reasons, they are really His children. When God spoke to His people about their children, He called them "*my* children," "the sons and daughters whom you have borne unto *me*" (Ezekiel 16:20-21). We do not have children only for our own benefit and ourselves—but for God! We nurture them and train them for Him.

Parenting is the highest calling God has given to mankind. Every other career is subservient to this one. Everything else we do in life serves our highest calling of teaching and training the next generation for God.

Finis Jennings Dake, in the *Dake's Annotated Reference Bible*, comments on Psalm 127:3-5, "Each child will in the process of time be a defense, support and propagation of the eternal reproduction of man and fulfillment of the plan of God for man. The more arrows one has, the more enemies he will slay, the more powerful will he be in the earth. The more children born and saved to help God administer the affairs of the eternal plan for man, the more reward God will have."

QUESTIONS

1. God says children are gifts. In the light of the Greek understanding of the word, *dechomal* (Matthew 18:5), how should we receive these gifts?

    _____

    _____

    _____

2. The Scriptures say God gives children for His service. Therefore, is it possible to hinder the purposes of God by not having the children He wants us to have? If so, why, and how?

    _____

    _____

    _____

3. Proverbs 30:15-16 tells us that the womb never says, "It is enough." What does this mean?

_____

_____

_____

4. God says that our children really belong to Him. How does this affect our parenting?

_____

_____

_____

CHAPTER 5

ᴀRROWS FOR GOD'S ARMY

G od calls our children arrows. Psalm 127:4-5 says, "As
arrows are in the hand of a mighty man; so are children
of the youth. *Happy* is the man that hath his quiver full of
them: they shall not be ashamed, but they shall speak with the
enemies in the gate."

In the context of Bible days, arrows were for the purpose
of war! We are in a war today and God needs arrows for His
army. God wants children born to fulfill His strategies and
plans. When a warrior went out to war, how many arrows
would he want in his quiver? One or two? No, he'd want to
squeeze in as many as he could. The more arrows he had in
his quiver, the more weapons he had to slay the enemy and the
more protection he provided for himself.

Have we forgotten God's Word that likens our children to
arrows? I have heard many people say, "I don't want to have
children because I don't want to bring children into this evil

world." But this is the very reason for having children. We train them to be the "light" and the "salt" in this dark world. We train and sharpen them to be "arrows" for God's army.

Satan hasn't forgotten God's Word. He knows that if he can limit the arrows from the Christian parents, he can limit the light that will expose his darkness. He can limit the truth that will expose his deceptions. He can limit the arrows that will destroy his works! Yes, the enemy is scared of the godly seed. He is out to destroy it by any means he can.

Satan, who comes "to steal, kill, and destroy," seeks to destroy newly formed life in the womb by abortion. But he has an even better plan than that—and it has been successful. He seeks to limit the godly seed before it is even conceived. By doing this, he limits the army of God. If the Christian Church had not listened to the humanistic lies of the enemy and limited their families, the army of God would be more powerful in this hour. The enemy's camp would be trembling. Instead they are laughing. Contraception has limited the army of God even more effectively than abortion.

Think about how many more pastors, prophets, teachers, and evangelists we would have. Think of how many more godly men and women in society there would be. Think of all the extra Christian families living in every street in every town in the nation—"sons of God, holding forth the word of life and shining like lights in the world" (Philippians 2:15,16). Just think of the increase of light exposing the darkness. Think of the arrows piercing the evil schemes of the enemy.

We have many enemies in the gates of our nation today. Where are the arrows to combat these enemies? We as the church have to bow our heads in shame as we see homosexuality and abortion and other evils flaunting in our gates. Oh, for more arrows to destroy these evil works.

Arrows do not just happen. It takes hours and hours of patience to straighten and sharpen an arrow that can effectively hit the mark. This is the task that God has given to parents. We are "arrow sharpeners," preparing arrows for God's army. The more "straight arrows" we prepare, the more we help God fulfill His plans on earth.

WHAT KIND OF ARROWS DOES GOD WANT US TO PREPARE?

There are different kinds of arrows mentioned in the Bible. Each one declares another aspect of the arrow that we need to work on as we sharpen our "arrows" to be ready to be used by God.

1. *Ready* arrows. Psalm 21:12, "Thou shalt make ready thine arrows upon thy strings…"

2. *Polished* arrows. Isaiah 49:2, "He made me a polished arrow; in His quiver hath He hid me; and said unto me, Thou art my servant, O Israel, in whom I will be glorified."

3. *Piercing* arrows. Numbers 24:8, "God shall pierce them through with His arrows."

4. *Scattering* arrows. 2 Samuel 22:5, Psalm 18:14, "He sent out His arrows, and scattered them…"

5. *Sticking fast* arrows. Psalm 38:2, "Thine arrows stick fast in me…"

6. *Sharp* arrows. Psalm 45:5, "Thine arrows are sharp…"

7. *Bright* arrows. Jeremiah 51:11a, "Make bright the arrows…"

8. *Light giving* arrows. Habakkuk 3:11, "At the light of thine arrows they went…"

9. *Going abroad* arrows. Psalm 77:17, "Thine arrows also went abroad."

10. *Destroying* arrows. Psalm 144:6, "Shoot out thine arrows, and destroy them."

11. *Hitting the mark* arrows. Jeremiah 50:9, "Their arrows shall be as of a mighty expert man, none shall return in vain."

12. *Shooting* arrows. Psalm 64:7; 144:6, "Shoot out thine arrows, and destroy them."

13. *On fire* arrows. Psalm 120:4, "Sharp arrows of the mighty, with coals of juniper."

14. *Delivering* arrows. 2 Kings 13:14-19, "The arrow of the Lord's deliverance."

Can you imagine the power of God that would be released in the nation with arrows like this?

Let's read together the story of Joash and Elisha in 2 Kings 13:14-19, which speaks of the delivering or victorious arrows. The Modern Language Bible version says, "Elisha said to him, 'Take a bow and arrows;' so he took a bow and arrows. Then he said to the king of Israel, 'Take hold of the bow.' He took hold of the bow, and Elisha put his hands on the hands of the king, saying, 'Open the window toward the east.' When he had opened it, Elisha said, 'Shoot!' and he shot. He exclaimed, '*The arrow of victory! The arrow of victory* over Syria! You shall utterly defeat Syria at Aphek.' Then he said, 'Take the arrows,' and he took them. 'Strike the ground with them,' he said to the king of Israel. So he struck it three times and then stopped. The man of God, displeased with him, said, 'You should have struck it five or six times, for then you would have kept on striking down Syria to its utter destruction. But you shall strike down Syria only three times.'

Elisha, the man of God, was angry with the king because he had no vision for totally defeating the enemy. In fact, Elisha died an angry man!

No wonder the enemy wants to hinder the birth of the godly seed. He knows that God wants them to be "arrows of victory" to defeat him. Many have stopped at two or three children and so we have missed out on many victories over the enemy, just like Joash did. If we had kept on having more arrows, we could have had more victories!

After our children had grown and left the nest, I remember lamenting to my daughter and son-in-law one night about how sad I felt that all the children were no longer at home and how I missed them all. He then rebuked me saying, "Mother, didn't you train them to be arrows to be sent forth across the world?" Yes, I needed reminding again!

MEN OF WAR

What kind of warriors did they train back in Bible days? We get an amazing picture as we read through the books of Kings and Chronicles. Let me pick out just a few Scriptures to give you a vision of the type of children God wants us to train for him.

They Were Skillful!

1 Chronicles 5:18, "The sons of Reuben, and the Gadites, and half the tribe of Manasseh, of valiant men, men able to bear buckler and sword, and to shoot with bow, and skillful in war, were four and forty thousand seven hundred and threescore, that went out to the war."

The word "skillful" in war is *lamad*. It means "educated, taught, and trained." What were they trained for? For war! We cannot live with our head in the sand. We are in a war. Our children must be trained for battle. They must be trained to stand and fight against the enemy of their souls. They must be trained to be warriors for God.

They Were Valiant!

1 Chronicles 7:2, "The sons of Tola... were valiant men of might in their generations."

This phrase, "in their generations," is repeated over and over again. They did not raise one or two valiant men. They raised generations of them. This is what God is looking for—a whole generation of warriors for Him who will fight against the enemy.

Now what is this word "valiant" that we read over and over again? It is the Hebrew word *chayil* that means "an army, virtue, valor, military strength, great forces, noble, strong."

1 Chronicles 7:11, "Mighty men of valor... fit to go out for war and battle."

1 Chronicles 9:13, "Very able men for the work of the service of the house of God."

1 Chronicles 12:8, "And of the Gadites there separated themselves unto David into the hold to the wilderness men of might, and men of war fit for the battle, that could handle shield and buckler, whose faces were like the faces of lions, and were as swift as the roes upon the mountains."

1 Chronicles 12:25, "Of the children of Simeon, mighty men of valor for the war."

1 Chronicles 12:28, "Zadok, a young man mighty of valor."

1 Chronicles 26:30, "Men of valor... in the service of the king."

1 Chronicles 26:32, "Men of valor... for every matter pertaining to God, and affairs of the king."

They Were Ready!

1 Chronicles 12:24, "The children of Judah that bare shield and spear were six thousand and eight hundred, ready armed to the war." They had been trained, polished and sharpened. They were ready for the battle!

They Were Expert!

1 Chronicles 12:33-36, "Expert in war."

They Were Choice!

1 Chronicles 7:40, "All these were the children of Asher, heads of their father's house, *choice* and mighty men of valor... And the number throughout the genealogy of them that were apt to the war and to battle was twenty and six thousand men."

Now let's look at the word "choice" in the above Scripture. It is the Hebrew word *barar* and it means "singled out, chosen, proved, cleansed, purified, and polished." Wow! Does that do something to you? What a vision! There is nothing greater that you could do in the whole of the universe than raise children like this—young men and women who are singled out by God, cleansed, purified, proved, and polished!

Our Daughters, Too!

"Just a minute," you say. "This is okay for our sons, but what about our daughters? Do they have to be valiant, too?" Yes. Look at Proverbs 31:10, "Who can find a virtuous woman, for her price is far above rubies." The word "virtuous" is *chayil*, the same word that is used for "valiant." God wants our daughters to be trained to be valiant and strong for Him, strong in virtue and morality, strong in faith, strong in truth, strong in convictions, prepared for motherhood and raising a family and strong to stand against the evil and deceptions of society.

ARE YOU A WARRIOR?

Unless you are a warrior, you cannot train warriors. Unless you understand the battle, how can you have a vision to raise "arrows?"

QUESTIONS

1. Why do you think that the Word of God says that the man who has his quiver *full* of arrows will be *happy*?

    _____

    _____

    _____

2. What is involved in making our "arrows" sharp and ready to be used for God?

    _____

    _____

    _____

3. Read the above Scriptures about arrows again and state the kind of arrows you want your children to be.

    _____

    _____

    _____

4. What do you think is a quiver full?

_____

_____

_____

CHAPTER 6

ℬUILD THE HOME AND LEAVE A LEGACY

How Do We Build?

The first desire of every married couple is to build or buy their own home. Let's look at what God says about building a home.

Ruth 4:11, "The Lord make the woman [Ruth] that is come into thine house like Rachel and like Leah, which two did build the house of Israel."

Psalm 127:1, "Except the Lord build the house, they labor in vain that build it."

Proverbs 14:1, "Every wise woman builds her house: but the foolish plucks it down with her hands."

Proverbs 9:1; 24:3-4, "Through wisdom is an house builded; and by understanding it is established: and by knowledge shall the chambers be filled with all precious and pleasant riches."

The Hebrew word for "build" is *banah*. There are three meanings contained in this word *banah*:

1. "To build up, to make, to set up surely." We understand this clearly. When we build a home, we want it to be on a strong foundation. We want everything about it to be solid. When we build our marriage, we also want it to be on a strong foundation, set surely on God's holy principles. That is why it is so important to search the Word of God to know His ways and His principles for marriage. Because God designed marriage, He is the only one who knows the true secrets for success.

2. "To repair." We also understand this. After we build a home, that is not the end of it. There is continual wear and tear and we have to regularly repair the leaks, the things that break and deteriorate. Similarly, it is one of the most important parts of the marriage relationship to watch out for the "little foxes" that come in to weaken and destroy our relationship. We must continually keep up the repair work. A house that is not regularly repaired will end up a "sorry sight." A marriage that is not constantly repaired will crumble.

3. "To obtain children, to bring about an increase in offspring." This is an unexpected meaning of the word *banah*, but it is very much part of it. We understand a little more of it in Deuteronomy 25:9 where it tells us what was to be done to the man who would not raise up seed to his brother's widow.

"Then shall his brother's wife come unto him in the presence of the elders, and loose his shoe from off his foot, and spit in his face, and shall answer and say, So shall it be done unto the man that will not build up [*banah*] his brother's house." We see that it means to "beget children."

Genesis 16:2, "Sarai said unto Abraham, Behold now, the Lord hath restrained me from bearing: I pray thee, go in unto my maid, it may be that I may obtain children [*banah*] by her." The Modern Language Bible translates it, "Go in to my maid; perhaps I may build up a family through her."

Genesis 30:3, "Rachel said, Behold my maid Bilhah, go in unto her; and she shall bear upon my knees, that I may also have children [*banah*] by her." In these two Scriptures, the Hebrew word *banah* is used again. How did Rachel and Leah build the house of Israel? By having children.

So we see that God says in His Word that having children is how we build a home and family. Do we plan our own family, or do we let the Lord choose? Remember, the Word says, "Except the Lord build the house, they labor in vain that build it."

Having children makes our home secure. It guarantees the future. Houses can be destroyed. Businesses can fail. But our children live to carry on our name and family lineage. God does not want us to think only of the present, but of the future. God's vision is to build godly generations. His plan is for parents to pass on His ways and principles to the next generation.

The greatest building program we can invest in is that of building godly generations. Philip Lancaster, editor of *Patriarch Magazine*, says: "Each man should aim to be the founder of a dynasty for God."

GOD IS INTERESTED IN GENERATIONS—PAST, PRESENT, AND FUTURE

When God spoke to the children of Israel, He confirmed the power of generational thinking. "I am the God of Abraham, Isaac, and Jacob"... "I am the God of thy fathers" is how He addressed them continually. Then He related the past to the future. When God spoke to Israel, He did not speak only to their present generation, but always included future generations. God's plan is for building a godly dynasty that will carry on down the generations.

Genesis 17:7-9, "I will establish my covenant between me and thee and *thy seed after thee in their generations* for an everlasting covenant, to be a God unto thee, and to *thy seed after thee*. And I will give unto thee, and to *thy seed after thee*, the land wherein thou art a stranger, all the land of Canaan, for an everlasting possession; and I will be their God. And God said unto Abraham, Thou shalt keep my covenant therefore, thou, and *thy seed after thee in their generations*." Notice that God is interested in the children that come after us!

Genesis 13:15 reveals how far God looks into the future generations, "For all the land which thou seest, to thee will I give it, and to thy seed *forever*." See also 2 Chronicles 20:7b; Jeremiah 25:5.

Deuteronomy 4:9-10, "Only take heed to thyself, and keep thy soul diligently, lest thou forget the things which thine eyes have seen, and lest they depart from thy heart all the days of thy life: but *teach them thy sons, and thy sons sons; that they may teach their children."*

The children of Israel also thought in the context of future generations. They did not only think of the "now." Joshua 22:27 says, "But that it may be a witness between us and you, and *our generations after us...* that your children may not say to our children *in time to come*, ye have no part in the Lord."

Deuteronomy 29:29, "Those things which are revealed belong unto us and to our children *forever."*

The following are further Scriptures to study on this subject. Now I know it is so easy to browse over this part without bothering to look up the Scriptures. However, I would encourage you to take the time to do this. As you look up these Scriptures, read them, meditate on them, and let the understanding of God's heart fill your vision, you will be mightily blessed. It is God's Word that will bless you, not man's words and ideas.

God is Concerned About the "Generations to Come"

Genesis 9:9,12; 12:1-7; 13:15; 17:7,9; 26:1-5; 28:11-14; Exodus 12:17,42; 13:8,14; 27:21; 29:42; 30:8,10,21; 31:13; 32: 13; Leviticus 3:17; 6:18; 7:36; 10:9; 17:7; 23:14,21,31,41; 24:3; Numbers 15:15,23; 25:11-13; 35:29; Deuteronomy 7:9; 29:22; 1 Chronicles 16:15; 28:8; 2 Chronicles 20:7; Ezra 9:12b; Psalm 71:18; 78:1-8; 100:5; 102:18; 105:8; Proverbs 13:22.

God Commands Us to Teach His Ways Diligently to Our Children and Grandchildren

Genesis 17:9; Deuteronomy 4:9-10; 4:21-24; 6:1-9, 20-25; 11:18-21; 31:19-21; 32:46-47; Psalm 45:17; 48:12-14; 71:18; 78:1-8; 79:13; 145:4-5; Proverbs 31:1; Isaiah 38:19; 59:21; Joel 1:3.

God Blesses the Future Generations of Righteous Parents

Genesis 9:9; 22:15-18; 26:1-5; 35:11-12; Exodus 20:5-6; 33:1; 34:6-7; Numbers 14:24; 25:10-13; Deuteronomy 1:8; 4:37,40; 5:10,29; 6:2-3; 7:7-10; 10:15; 11:19-21; 12:25,28; 28:1-14; 29:29; 30:19; 2 Samuel 22:51; 1 Kings 2:33; 2 Kings 10:30; 15:12; 1 Chronicles 28:8; Ezra 9:12; Psalm 14:5b; 25:12-13; 37:25-26; 102:28; 103:17-18; 106:30-31; 112:1-2; 128:1-6; 132:11-12; Proverbs 20:7; Isaiah 44:1-3; 61:9; 65:17,25; Jeremiah 35:18-19; Luke 1:50; Acts 2:38-39; 3:25.

CHILDREN CARRY ON YOUR NAME

It is important to have children to carry on the family name and build the godly dynasty. This is why God provided the levirate marriage, so that if a brother died and had no children, the next brother could take his brother's widow and raise up seed for him so "that his name may not be blotted out of Israel" (Deuteronomy 25:6). God puts importance on the family name.

He promises Israel in Isaiah 66:22, "For as the new heavens and the new earth, which I will make, shall remain before me, saith the Lord, so shall your seed and *your name remain.*"

When Jacob blessed Ephraim and Manasseh, he put his name, his father's name, and his grandfather's name upon them! Genesis 48:16, "The Angel which redeemed me from all evil, bless the lads; and let my name be named on them, and the name of my fathers Abraham and Isaac; and let them grow into a multitude in the midst of the earth."

We have found that it is not as easy as you would think to carry on the family name. We are currently blessed with twenty-one grandchildren (and have two more on the way), but it took fifteen grandchildren before we got one to carry on the family name! What about families who only have one or two children? Sadly, many family names are dying out today.

We read an interesting Scripture in Deuteronomy 33:6 where Moses blesses each tribe of Israel. Speaking of Reuben, he says, "Let Reuben live and not die out." Reuben was the firstborn, the beginning of Jacob's strength, but because he sinned greatly by sleeping with his father's concubine, he did not receive the fullness of blessings he should have received. However, God states here that He does not want his name to die out.

While still living in my native country of New Zealand, I heard about the "Cousin" family. The parents, who had nine children, did not believe in God. The three boys married but never had any children. The six girls never married. There were no grandchildren, no nephews or nieces. And sadly there were no more cousins! A family name died out because they had no vision for family. On the other hand, consider the spiritual and practical benefits of bearing children:

To bear children ensures that your name continues.

To bear and raise godly children is to build a home that will affect the destiny of the nation.

To raise godly children is to leave a legacy for future generations. The legacy of homes, land, and wealth is great, but these can be destroyed and vanish away. The legacy of children will last through the generations.

To bear children is to lay up treasure in Heaven. God is not only interested in populating earth, but in populating eternity. Parenthood has eternal rewards. It is not something that fades away. It lasts into the generations to come and also eternity. We need to guard ourselves from the trends of our day that lure our attention to "things" that will not last and pull us away from the tasks that are lasting, such as raising children.

LAYING THE FOUNDATION FOR FUTURE GENERATIONS

Back in 1900, a trace was done on offspring of the Jonathan and Sarah Edwards family. Jonathan Edwards was a theologian, pastor, missionary, and university president. He had a brilliant mind. At age ten he entered Yale College and at sixteen years he graduated at the head of his class. When he was twenty-three-years old, he became pastor of the church at Northampton, Massachusetts, which at the time was the most influential church in America. That same year he married Sarah Pierrepont, a daughter of one of the founders of Yale, and they had twelve children.

By 1900, this godly marriage had produced:

13 college presidents;
65 professors;
100 lawyers and a dean of an outstanding law school;
30 judges;
60 doctors and a dean of a medical school;
80 holders of public office including 3 United States Senators;
3 mayors of large cities;
3 state governors;
A Vice President of the United States; and
a Controller of United States Treasury.

They entered the ministry in platoons, sent one-hundred missionaries overseas as well as staffing many mission boards. Members of the family wrote 135 books and edited eighteen journals and periodicals.

Nearly another century has gone by since this study. How much more has this one family influenced the nation? This happened because one husband and wife had a vision for raising a godly seed and building a godly dynasty.

I'm sure you've heard of William and Catherine Booth who were the founders of the Salvation Army. They had eight children and were faithful to train them for God. Every one of those eight children served God in a mighty way. We named one of our daughters, Evangeline Faith, after Evangeline Booth, one of their daughters, who was a great evangelist. Not only did they train their children, but the foundation of their godly training continued into the following generations. They had forty-five grandchildren and every one of them also served God with all their hearts, many on the mission field. And their great-grandchildren continued as missionaries.

I have some dear friends in Australia who presently have nine children, but are hoping for ten. The mother has always had a vision to raise ten children who will shine as lights in the nation. Recently she shared with me her total vision. If she has ten children and each of her children have ten children, and their children have ten children, she will end up with one-thousand great-grandchildren! Now isn't that a great vision? What far reaching influences a godly mother can have, not only in determining the destiny of a nation, but also future generations.

QUESTIONS

1. What do you think it means when God says that He "formed man" (Genesis 2:7) but he "built" [*banah*] (Genesis 2:22) the woman? What is your understanding?

_____

_____

_____

2. In the light of the full understanding of the world "build" [*banah*], and in the context of family which is the theme of Psalm 127 and 128, state what you think the following Scripture means: "Except the Lord build the house, they labor in vain that build it."

_____

_____

_____

BE FRUITFUL AND MULTIPLY

3. How do we successfully pass on the baton of God's truth to the coming generation?

_____

_____

_____

4. God's plan is for godly dynasties. Discuss together or write down your answers to the following questions in light of the above Scriptures.

   a. What plans do you have for building a godly dynasty and establishing your family name for the generations to come?

   _____

   _____

   _____

b. What plans do you have for diligently teaching your children and your children's children God's ways?

_____

_____

_____

c. How do you intend to give your children a sense of roots and origin and relate their past generations to the present?

_____

_____

_____

d. What kind of a legacy are you leaving for the future?

_____

_____

_____

$\mathcal{T}$HE NATURAL FUNCTION

Created to Mother

Women have been physically created by God to mother. God gave them the gift of womb and breasts. These are the most distinguishing characteristics of women. God designed a wondrous reproductive system that He has creatively put in every woman—in fact, even before birth. When a little baby girl is being formed in the secret place of the womb, God is busy preparing her for motherhood. By the third month of gestation, the reproductive organs already contain a few primitive eggs and by the time of birth there are more than a million! Medical books vary in their estimation of primordial egg cells at the time of birth from 250,000 to one to two million. A pretty good preparation for motherhood, don't you think?

When Adam saw the woman that God created for him, He said, "She shall be called Woman, because she was taken out of man" (Genesis 2:21-23). Webster's 1828 Dictionary explains that the word "woman" is a combination of the words "'womb" and "man." Woman means "womb man" or "man with a womb." The Chinese translation for womb is "the palace of a child." The purpose of the womb is to nurture life. Breasts are designed to nurse babies.

It is true that the breast is also for delight and lovemaking. The word for breast in Proverbs 5:19, "Let her breasts satisfy thee at all times," is the Hebrew word *dad* which means "love token." But the primary purpose is for nursing.

The most common Greek word for women in the New Testament is *gune*. It means, "woman, wife." Only twice is a different word used. This word *thelus* comes from the root word *thele*, which means "nipple, to suckle, to nurse, to mother." It is a picture of the woman created with breasts and womb to function as God intended. Where does God use these words?

1. Matthew 19:4, "Have ye not read, that He which made them at the beginning made them male and female [*thelus*]." Jesus uses this word to describe how women were created in the beginning.

2. Romans 1:26-27, "For this cause God gave them up until vile affections: for even their women [*thelus*] did change the natural use into that which is against nature..." Why did God use the full revelation of motherhood, including the function of the breasts, in this passage? Because God wants women to function as He created them. Women were created by God's design to function as nourishers by nourishing life in their womb and a

babe at their breast. When women deliberately turn away from their natural functions, they do it to their own detriment.

Romans 9:19-20 asks, "Who art thou that disputest against God? Shall the thing formed say to him that formed it, Why hast thou made me thus?" To ignore the way we were designed and created by God can only be foolish.

More statistics are constantly coming to hand to prove that the more a mother breastfeeds, the less likelihood she has of getting breast cancer, ovarian cancer, or even fibroids and endometriosis. Here are a few quotes:

Reported in the *Science News*, October 1992, by Kathy Facelmann, Malcolm C. Pike from the Southern California School of Medicine, Los Angeles, "blames the epidemic rates of breast and other female cancers on a fact of modern life: The average American woman starts menstruating at age 12 and typically gives birth to one or two infants. Pike estimates she will ovulate a whopping 450 times during her lifetime. By contrast, a woman who lived 200 years ago would have started menstruating at age 17 and would have delivered and breastfed about eight babies. Thus our foremothers ovulated fewer than 150 times during their lives. Pike argues that pregnancy and lactation provide a crucial resting period for the ovaries, the female sex glands that produce not only eggs, but also several powerful hormones, including estrogen and progesterone. Each month, a woman's body readies itself for pregnancy. The ovaries secrete estrogen and progesterone, which tell the breast cells to begin dividing in preparation for milk production. In years past, women went through this cycle less frequently because they were more often either pregnant or breastfeeding."

"Women who have a full pregnancy before the age of 18 have one third the breast cancer risk of a woman whose first child is delayed until after age 30, or never has a child. One interesting angle on the breastfeeding issue is that the Tania women in Hong Kong, who traditionally only nurse with their right breast, have more cancer in their left breast" (Mark Renneker, M.D, *Understanding Cancer*).

A recent CASH study involving about nine-thousand women revealed that the women with the least breast cancer were those who had the most children and thus a longer breastfeeding experience. CASH researcher Peter Layde, M.D. reports, "We found that women who breastfed a total of two years or more had nearly a third less breast cancer than women who did not breast feed."

Lamentations 4:3 says, "Even jackals offer their breasts to nurse their young, but my people have become heartless like ostriches in the desert."

Studies also reveal that women who bear their first child before age twenty-two are less likely than others to develop ovarian cancer. Those who delay pregnancy are more prone to have endometriosis which is known as the "career woman's disease." God knows this and says in Psalm 127:4, "As arrows are in the hand of a mighty man, so are children of the *youth*." God knows what is right. God wants children to be born in our youth.

The Word of God is always ahead of science. Look at the following Scriptures and we see how God, who created women, wants them to function:

1. 1 Timothy 2:14-15, "Adam was not deceived, but the woman being deceived was in the transgression. Notwithstanding she shall be saved in childbearing, if they continue in faith and love and holiness with sobriety."

The word for childbearing is *teknogonia*. This means more than the act of childbirth. It is the career of childbearing. A breakdown of the word is as follows:

teknon	"child"
gonia	is from a root word *gen* "to beget"

Vine's Exposition of Greek Words says it "denotes bearing children, implying the duties of motherhood."

Other translations say: "But she will be *saved through motherhood...*" (NAB). "Women will find their *salvation in motherhood*" (TCNT).

The context of this Scripture denotes that this is not talking about salvation from sin, but salvation from deception. Women will be saved from getting into deception and from being lured away from their divine destiny, if they continue to walk in the role of motherhood which God planned for them.

We often hear the familiar comment that the sexual union is not just for the purpose of childbearing but also for pleasure. Yes, it is true that God planned the sexual union to be delightful and pleasurable. I wonder if God made it so pleasurable to ensure fruitfulness. He understands our human nature. If it wasn't so wonderful, we wouldn't bother and there would be no fruitfulness. It is an interesting fact that God created the woman to desire her husband sexually the most during the time of ovulation, which is her most fertile time. Why did God plan this? Because He desires fruitfulness.

2. 1 Timothy 5:14, "I will therefore that the younger women marry, bear children [*teknogonea*, verb], guide the house, give none occasion to the adversary to speak reproachfully." The same Greek word is used again in this Scripture.

3. 1 Timothy 5:9-10, "Well reported of for good works; if she has brought up [*teknotropheo*] children, if she has lodged strangers, if she has washed the saints' feet, if she has relieved the afflicted, if she has diligently followed every good work." "Brought up" is the Greek word *teknotropheo*. *Teknon* means "child;" *tropho* means "to cherish, to nourish." The full meaning is "to be a child nourisher."

This godly woman firstly embraced her motherhood. This was her number one career. It was her top priority in life. She willingly received the children God gave to her. Nurturing and nourishing children was her greatest delight and she embraced it with joy.

We notice that her mother heart was even bigger than her immediate family. Her nurturing heart reached out into the community. She was a nourisher of all who needed her care. She looked beyond her own needs to reach out to the needs of others. She opened her home in hospitality. She ministered to the needy. No task was too lowly to help someone in need. She walked in the fullness of motherhood and the destiny that God has planned for women.

THE UNSATISFIED WOMB

It saddens my heart when I hear of husbands who refuse to allow their wives to have more children even when they long to do so. Unfortunately, they are ignorant of the intense longing and desire a woman can have to nurture a child in her womb. The Word of God, which is God's eternal truth and has all understanding on every matter, states that the womb never says, "It is enough." Proverbs 30:15,16 says, "There are three things that are never satisfied, yea, four things say not, It is enough: The grave; and the barren womb; the earth that is not filled with water; and the fire that saith not, It is enough."

Mothers who have felt the desperate longing for another child can understand the cry of Rachel's heart. Genesis 30:1 says, "When Rachel saw that she bare Jacob no children, Rachel envied her sister; and said unto Jacob, Give me children, or else I die."

NATURAL FAMILY PLANNING

We mentioned earlier in this chapter that God created the wife to desire sexual relations with her husband especially during the time of ovulation, which is the most fertile time. Natural Family Planning (NFP) avoids having relations at this time so that conception cannot take place.

Couples who are rightly troubled by the implications of artificial contraceptives often turn to NFP as an alternative form of child prevention. It is a morally superior form of contraception because it neither sets out to destroy the sperm, which contains life and therefore the potential of future human beings, nor is it an abortifacient. Having said this, I believe we must be honest that NFP is not completely "natural." First, it denies the wife the intimacy she would naturally desire with her husband. Second, it is a deliberate attempt to thwart God's natural design for intimacy in which the potential for life and the act of love are mutually inextricable throughout the fertile season of a woman's life. For these reasons we must conclude that NFP contradicts God's natural order for divine creation and His stated will that we be fruitful and multiply. On the other hand, Scripture does indicate that the children of Israel were to practice sexual abstinence during seasons of uncleanness and physical recovery, and that Paul directed husbands and wives to practice abstinence for a season during times of marital stress. In both cases, the reasons for abstinence were unrelated to child prevention.

More information on NFP can be obtained from reading *The Art of Natural Family Planning* by John and Sheila Kippley. Available from: The Couple to Couple League, P.O. Box 111184, Cincinnati, OH 45211-1184, www.ccli.org.

For further understanding of how breastfeeding can naturally space your family, read the book, *Breastfeeding and Natural Child Spacing: How Breastfeeding Spaces Babies* by Sheila Kippley. Available from The Couple to Couple League. P.O. Box 111184, Cincinnati, OH 45211-1184, www.ccli.org.

QUESTIONS

1. Explain what it means to be "saved through motherhood."

    _____

    _____

    _____

2. Why is it important that a mother seeks to breastfeed her baby?

    _____

    _____

    _____

3. How do you think it affects our Creator God, when we decide to cut off our reproduction, which He so intricately designed?

    _____

    _____

    _____

4. What are some of the ways women can turn from their "natural function?"

_____

_____

_____

CHAPTER 8

$\mathcal{T}$RUST AND OBEY

To Obey is Better Than Sacrifice

A number of couples have said to me, "We have sacrificed having more children because we want to be free to serve God." That sounds very zealous and commendable and these precious couples are very sincere. But is this God's perfect will? God tells us plainly that He requires obedience before sacrifice.

1 Samuel 15:22-23, "Hath the Lord as great delight in burnt offerings and sacrifices, as in *obeying* the voice of the Lord? Behold to *obey* is better than sacrifice, and to hearken than the fat of rams."

It seems that many couples would do any sacrifice for God rather than obey God's first commandment. They would rather obey any commandment than this one. I have meditated much on this subject, seeking to know God's heart and mind. As I was wrestling with this truth one night, God woke me up with these words ringing in my heart: "The perfect will of God for your life will never contradict His existing commandments."

The perfect will of God for our lives will never contradict the truths that God has established in His Word. The book of Genesis is the book of beginnings. The truths that are written in Genesis are never altered throughout the rest of the Bible, only enlarged upon.

The first principle God gave in the first chapter of the first book of the Bible to "Be fruitful and multiply and replenish the earth" is unchanging. It is an established law for this earth. It has never been withdrawn. In this manual we have continued to read so many Scriptures that build upon this foundational truth. Therefore, to deliberately disobey this command, or to abandon this commandment in order to do service for God, is not God's perfect will.

We cannot disobey one commandment in order to fulfill other commandments.

Could Jeremiah 7:28 be a testimony of the nations today? "This is a nation that obeys not the voice of the Lord their God." Will we be those who will follow God's ways—or go our own way?

Our Own Way

Proverbs 3:5-6 tells us to not rely on our own understanding. Our own understanding is not strong enough to lean on or put the whole weight of our lives upon. It will bend and break. When we lean to our own understanding, we lean to what suits us and our particular circumstances. We lean toward selfishness. We lean toward the easy way out.

Although we may feel that "our way" is best for us now, it is not always the best in the long run. Obedience to God's ways, even when we feel they don't suit us and it is contrary to everything we want to do, will always lead us to the ultimate blessing. Proverbs 28:26 says, "He that trusts in His own heart is a fool" and Isaiah 5:21 says, "Woe unto them that are wise in their own eyes, and prudent in their own sight!" The following are further Scriptures that speak about choosing our own way:

Numbers 15:39b; Deuteronomy 12:8; Judges 2:19b; Psalm 5:10; 81:11-12; 106:39; Proverbs 1:30,31; 3:5-7; 12:15; 14:12,14; 20:24; 21:2; 23:4; 26:5,12; 28:26; 30:12; Isaiah 5:21; 53:6; 56:11b; 58:13-14; 65:2b; 66:3b; Jeremiah 8:6; 9:13-15; 10:23; 18:11-12; 23:17-26; Ezekiel 13:3, 22:31; 36:17,31-32; Hosea 10:6b; 13:2; Philippians 2:21.

God's Way

God's ways are contrary to our natural way of thinking. They are usually opposite to the current trend of society. We belong to a different kingdom with different principles.

Isaiah 55:8-9, "For My thoughts are not your thoughts, neither are your ways my ways, saith the Lord. For as the heavens are higher than the earth, so are my ways higher than your ways, and my thoughts than your thoughts." Whose ways are we going to choose?

Deuteronomy 10:12, "What doth the Lord thy God require of thee... but to walk in *all his ways.*"

His ways are the only ways that bring peace. They are the only ways that lead to success. They are the only ways that will accomplish God's purposes.

Further Scriptures about choosing God's ways: Psalm 18: 30,32; 25:12; 32:8; 81:13-16; 86:11; 119:3,14-15,27,30,32-33; 128:1; Proverbs 3:5-8; Isaiah 2:3; Zechariah 3:7; John 5:30; 6: 38; 1 Corinthians 3:20.

UP TO ZION—DOWN TO EGYPT!

We do not need to go to "Egypt" (which is a type of the world) for our counsel. We will find all the truth we need to know in the Word of God. It is all there if we will take time to seek it out. How easily we succumb to the way of the world. May God help us to stand strong in His truth and totally trust in His counsel, even if it is not the popular trend. When we trust in the world's wisdom, we are on a downward path.

Isaiah 30:1-3 says, "Woe to the rebellious children, saith the Lord, that take counsel, but not of Me... that walk to go *down* into Egypt, and have not asked at my mouth; to strengthen themselves in the strength of Pharaoh, and to trust in the shadow of Egypt. Therefore shall the strength of Pharaoh be your shame, and the trust in the shadow of Egypt your confusion."

Isaiah 31:1,3, "Woe to them that go *down* to Egypt for help; and stay on horses, and trust in chariots, because they are many; and in horsemen, because they are very strong; but they look not unto the Holy One of Israel, neither seek the Lord...."

Now the Egyptians are men, and not God; and their horses flesh, and not spirit."

When we trust in worldly advice, "because they are many" and it is the popular opinion, it will eventually bring us to shame. When we go *down* to Egypt, we walk further away from the light of God's truth and further into confusion. The Scriptures always speak of going *up* to Zion (e.g., Isaiah 2:3, Jeremiah 31:6) but *down* to Egypt. (When you are in Israel, you always refer to going *up* to Jerusalem, even if you are in the north of the country. If you want to walk the "upward way," trust in God's unchanging truth rather than the humanistic doctrines of this age.

When God delivered the children of Israel from Egypt, He told them that they were "*never to return to Egypt again*" (Deuteronomy 17:16). When God delivers us from the kingdom of darkness, He does not want us to return to that kingdom again either. We don't have to look to the world for our counsel any longer. We now have a higher source—God's infallible Word that will never lie or fail us. It will always be in opposition to the world system, but "Let God be true, but every man a liar" (Romans 3:4). This is where the crunch comes. This is where persecution arises. Whose advice are we going to obey? Who will we put our faith in—God or man?

OBEY WITH A WILLING HEART

Mary is a beautiful example. God chose this unknown virgin to bring forth His precious Son. He chose her because she was a willing vessel. God is looking for fathers and mothers with obedient hearts who will welcome to their hearts the children whom God has planned to send them. He is looking for those who have the same spirit Mary had when she said, "Be it unto me according to thy Word." She was totally surrendered to the will of the Lord. In the face of poverty, ridicule, rejection, and estrangement, she embraced the perfect will of God.

Can we say from our hearts, "Be it unto me according to thy word?"

Psalm 110:3, "Thy people shall be willing in the day of thy power." Willing and obedient hearts are a prerequisite for restoration and revival.

Isaiah 1:19, "If ye be willing and obedient, ye shall eat the good of the land."

OBEY GOD RATHER THAN MAN

Society conditions us to its mold. Nobody wants to be different. Everyone wants to do what everyone else is doing. Today's pattern is to limit the number of children in a family, so most people, Christians included, follow suit. Population controllists seek to limit families to no more than two children per family. The pressure is on.

One of the heartaches I hear from young mothers all over the world is that their parents do not want them to have more children. When I speak at conferences, I constantly hear these complaints. I read them in the letters that pour in every day:

"Use your head. That's what God gave you brains for!"

"Please don't have a baby until you complete your Ph.D."

"You don't need another baby, you already have a son and daughter."

But whom do we obey? God or man? Acts 5:29 says, "We ought to obey God rather than men."

OBEY TO BE SAVED FROM DECEPTION

John 8:31-32, "If you *obey* what I say, then you are really my disciples… you will know the truth and the truth will set you free." I have always loved quoting this Scripture, but it was only recently that I noticed the context in which it was written. The bottom line is that we will know the truth if we walk in obedience. If we don't, we can be led into deception.

Disobedience leads to deception. Obedience leads to truth!

OBEY TO BE BLESSED

Obedience is always related to blessing.

Genesis 22:15-18, "In thy seed shall all the nations of the earth be blessed; *because thou hast obeyed my voice.*"

Genesis 26:4-5, "I will make thy seed to multiply as the stars of heaven…. *because* that Abraham *obeyed my voice*, and kept my charge, my commandments, my statutes, and my laws."

BE FRUITFUL AND MULTIPLY

Deuteronomy 4:40, "Thou shalt *keep his statutes*, and his commandments... *that it may go well with thee*, and with thy children after thee...." (Also see Deuteronomy 5:16,29,33; 6:2,3,18.

Deuteronomy 28:1-14, "If thou shalt hearken diligently unto the voice of the Lord thy God, to observe and to do all His commandments... *all these blessings shall come on thee, and overtake thee.*"

Isaiah 48:17-19, "Thus saith the Lord, thy Redeemer, the Holy One of Israel; I am the Lord thy God which teacheth thee to profit, which leadeth thee by the way that thou shouldest go. *O that thou hadst hearkened to my commandments!* Then had thy peace been as a river, and thy righteousness as the waves of the sea: Thy seed also had been as the sand, and the offspring of thy bowels like the gravel thereof."

Jeremiah 7:23-24, "Obey My voice, and I will be your God, and ye shall be my people: and walk ye in all the ways that I have commanded you, *that it may be well unto you.*"

The truth of the old hymn still stands:

Trust and obey, for there's no other way
To be happy in Jesus, but to trust and obey.

QUESTIONS

1. List the promises that God gives to those who obey Him and His commands:

    a. Exodus 15:26.
        We will have no _____.

    b. Exodus 20:6; Deuteronomy 5:10; Psalm 103:17-18.
        We will receive _____.

    c. Deuteronomy 4:40; 5:29,33; 6:17-18; 12:28;
        Jeremiah 7:23; 42:6.
        It will go _____ with us.

    d. Leviticus 25;18; 26:3-5.
        We will live in _____ _____.

    e. Leviticus 26:3,6.
        God will give us _____.

    f. Leviticus 26:3,9; Deuteronomy 6:3; 7:11-14; 13:
        17b,18; 28:4; 3, 9,10,16.
        We will be _____ and _____.

    g. Leviticus 26:3,11-12; 1 John 3:24.
        We will experience the _____ _____.

    h. Deuteronomy 4:5-6.

We will have _____ and _____.

i. Deuteronomy 6:1-2; 11:8-9,21.
   We will have a _____.

j. Exodus 19:5.
   We will be a _____ to the Lord.

k. Deuteronomy 26:16-19; 28:1.
   He will set us on _____.

l. Exodus 23:20-22; Leviticus 26:3,7-8; Deuteronomy
   11:22-23; 28:7.
   God will deal with our _____.

m. Deuteronomy 11:26-28; Deuteronomy 28:1-14;
   Psalm 119:2; Proverbs 8:32; Luke 11:28.
   We will be _____.

n. Leviticus 26:3-5,10; Deuteronomy 28:5,8a; Isaiah 1:
   19.
   We will have provision of _____.

o. Deuteronomy 28:11a.
   We will have _____.

p. Deuteronomy 28:13.
   We will be the _____ and not the tail.

q. Deuteronomy 28:13.
We will be _____ _____ and not beneath.

r. 1 Chronicles 22:13.
We will _____.

s. Psalm 19:11.
We will receive_____.

t. Psalm 112:1-2a.
Our children will be _____.

u. Psalm 119:6.
We will not be _____.

v. Proverbs 29:18.
We will be _____.

w. John 14:23.
God will _____ with us.

x. John 15:10.
We will_____.

y. John 15:14.
He will call us His _____.

z. 1 John 3:22.
We will receive _____.

2. With what attitude does God want us to obey His commandments?

    a.   Deuteronomy 6:17; 11:22; Psalm 119:4; Zechariah 6: 15.

       _____

    b.   Deuteronomy 26:16; Psalm 119:33-34,69.

       _____

    c.   Psalm 119:44,117.

       _____

    d.   Psalm 119:60.

       _____

    e.   Psalm 119:16,47.

       _____

3. What happens when we trust in our own counsel?

    a. Judges 2:19-20. We will receive the_____

        _____

    b. Psalm 5:10. We will _____

        _____

    c. Psalm 106:39; Ezekiel 36:17. We will be _____

        _____

    d. Proverbs 14:14. We will ____ _____

        _____

    e. Proverbs 26:12; 28:26; 1 Cor 3:19. We are a _____

        _____ ____

4. Why do you think disobedience can lead to deception?

    _____

    _____

    _____

CHAPTER 9

GOD'S PROVISION
Walk in Faith

"How can I afford to have more children?" you ask. This is certainly a valid question if we trust in our own resources. But if we trust in God, we need have no fears.

The Bible teaches that we are to look to God in faith not only for children, but for His provision for these children conceived in faith. The argument I often hear that preventing children is "good stewardship" is foreign to the Bible. Such thinking may appear to some to be "common sense," but it is certainly not biblical sense. The idea that having children is a function of one's personal economics is contrary to the patterns and principles which the Scriptures do reveal. If anything, the Bible teaches that those who are economically poor should desire more children, because with such children come all sorts of blessings including economic blessings. But to understand these truths we must come to the Lord in faith believing He is a God who cares for His own.

Many of us have forgotten what it means to walk the Christian life of faith. Colossians 2:6 says, "As ye have therefore received Christ Jesus the Lord, so walk ye in Him." How did we receive Christ Jesus into our lives? By faith. How should we continue to walk our new life in Christ Jesus? Also by faith. Remember, "Whatsoever is not of faith, is sin." Romans 14:23.

We confess that we are "children of Abraham." Abraham walked by faith. Are we truly "children of Abraham" in experience? Hebrews 11:8-10 says, "By faith Abraham, when he was called to go out into a place which he should after receive for an inheritance, *obeyed*; and he went out, not knowing whither he went...." What was Abraham's faith? When He heard the word of the Lord, he *obeyed*. It was simple obedience. But it took faith to obey that word. He did not know where he was going. He had to leave his home and comforts. But he put his trust in God and obeyed. That's the simple faith that we are to walk in.

When God says, "Be fruitful and multiply," faith obeys.

Unbelief says...

"But how will I provide for these children?"
"But we only live in an apartment, we haven't built our own home yet."
"But we haven't got a big enough home."
"But if we have more than two children, we won't be able to afford their college education."

Faith simply obeys—and trusts God!

Recently I received a letter from a mother of seven children. This family of nine lived in a two-bedroom, 784 square foot trailer home. Did she write with grumbling and complaints? No, her letter was full of the blessings and joys of their family life. She says, "We are blessed, and are managing, because we are grateful for what God has provided. We often laugh when we think of the family we bought our trailer from. They had one small boy and felt they needed more space! I guess it is all in how one looks at it! We heat totally with wood and appreciate the warmth and coziness. I must add, it is also practical on a day like today. We are experiencing a blizzard. Many inches of thick, white snow keep us closed in. The telephone quit and electricity is still out. We are having a ball—melting snow, simmering soup, playing board games, writing letters, and cleaning cupboards. Perhaps tonight it will be a lamplight eve. The children love that...." This family doesn't sound as though they are deprived, do they?

For nearly a year our daughter lived in a one-room cabin with no running water, no bathroom, and no inside kitchen. She had five children and was pregnant with her sixth. They now have a bathroom, a kitchen, running water, another room added on—and their seventh baby! But they still don't have bedrooms or even beds for the children. There's no room for beds. Each night the children take their blankets from the big pile in the corner and make their cozy spot on the floor in the all-purpose room. Is Evangeline a grumbling mess? No! Are the children deprived? No! They all have a wonderful life. She is the most joyful mother in this nation. The children are happy and live adventure-filled lives. Some time ago, some young people gathered together and began to discuss who were the richest people they knew. They all came to the conclusion that Evangeline and Howard were the richest! It had nothing to do with their material possessions. It had all to do with their joy of the Lord and their attitude to life.

Another one of my daughters believes that children save you money! A bigger family teaches you how to be more frugal. If you don't have children or only one or two, you usually become more materialistic; you go out to dinner more and you buy more "things" that you don't really need. We definitely don't need to have all the things that we think we do.

BELIEVE GOD'S PROMISES

How many children did Abraham believe for? One? I thought so, until I re-read the Scripture. I will quote part, but read the whole story in Genesis 15:1-6. "And he brought him forth abroad, and said, Look now toward Heaven, and tell the stars, if thou be able to number them: and he said unto him, So shall thy seed be. And he believed in the Lord; and he counted it to him for righteousness." Abraham believed God for a family as many as the stars of the heaven, as the dust of the earth, and as the sand upon the seashore—and God counted it to him for righteousness.

Deuteronomy 28:4-6,8,11-12. "Blessed shall be the fruit of thy body, *and* the fruit of thy ground, and the fruit of thy cattle, the increase of thy cattle, and the flocks of thy sheep. Blessed shall be thy basket and thy store..."

It is interesting to note that *before* God says He will bless the fruit of our ground, our basket, and store, He says He will bless the fruit of our body.

When He blesses the fruit of our body, *then* He blesses our ground, our cattle, and our storehouse, so we will have enough to feed and provide for the blessings He gives us from the fruit of our body! Simple, isn't it? Many have small families because they think they would not be able to feed and clothe more children. But God will bless us according to how we are blessed from the fruit of our body! His blessing of provision is to provide for the ultimate blessing of children! Isn't that a wonderful revelation? God wouldn't need to bless our land, our cattle, and bless us with extra food if there was no one to give it to.

To reassure us, He repeats the same promise again in verses 10-13, "And the Lord shall make thee plenteous in goods, in the fruit of thy body, *and* in the fruit of thy cattle, and in the fruit of thy ground...." This is stated again in Deuteronomy 7: 13-14.

If we only have faith for a small family, we will receive small provision. If we have faith to believe God for the children He wants us to have, we will experience God's larger provision to provide for them. God's provision is for the "fruit of the womb." And remember that God does not show up with

His provision before the baby comes. He will show up when the new baby arrives. And He never fails!

We see this theme reiterated in Ezekiel 36:8-10 where the prophet speaks about preparing for the return of the Jews to their homeland. "O mountains of Israel, you shall shoot forth your branches, and yield your fruit to my people of Israel; for they are at hand to come." These "heavy crops of fruit," as The Living Bible translates it, were for the purpose of feeding people!

Nehemiah 9:19-21, "Forty years didst Thou sustain them in the wilderness, so that *they lacked nothing*; their clothes waxed not old, and their feet swelled not."

They did not live in palatial houses—they lived in temporary tents! They did not have two cars per family. They did not have all the modern conveniences we have today. But God said they *"lacked nothing."* This will also be our experience as we trust in our God. Read also Deuteronomy 2:7b.

Psalm 37:25, "I have been young, and now am old; yet have I not seen the righteous forsaken, nor his seed begging bread."

Matthew 6:25-34, "Therefore I say to you, do not worry about your life, what you will eat or what you will drink; nor about your body, what you will put on. Is not life more than food and the body more than clothing?... So why do you worry about clothing? Consider the lilies of the field, how they grow: they neither toil nor spin: and yet I say to you that even Solomon in all his glory was not arrayed like one of these. Now if God so clothes the grass of the field, which today is, and tomorrow is thrown into the oven, will he not much more clothe you, O you of little faith? Therefore do not worry, saying, 'What shall we eat?' or 'What shall we drink?' or 'What shall we wear?'... For your heavenly Father knows that you need all these things. But seek first the kingdom of God and His righteousness, and all these things shall be added to you."

Philippians 4:19, "My God shall supply all your need according to His riches in glory by Christ Jesus."

JESUS' EXAMPLE

Let's look at our greatest example, Jesus Himself. He was born in a manger in a barn with the animals. Jesus was born to be King, but God did not provide a palace for His Son in which to be born. There was no beautifully draped cradle with lace and frills. Only straw!

Isn't it amazing that God chose to bring forth His beloved Son through the process of birth. He could have sent Him down from Heaven on a chariot of fire! He could have had a legion of angels escort Him from the majesty of heaven. But no! He chose for Jesus to be conceived and nurtured in a womb, to be born of a woman, the way that God planned for all human life to come into this world. Surely this raises birth to a high estate. What a privilege to give birth and give life to children, the same way that Jesus came into the world!

After the days of a mother's purification, Mary took her baby to the temple to be dedicated. The parents were to bring a lamb to be sacrificed for the dedication. However, if they could not afford a lamb, they were to bring two turtle doves or young pigeons (Leviticus 12:6-8). The account in Luke 2:23-24 tells us that Joseph and Mary brought doves or pigeons. They were the poorer class. They couldn't afford to bring a lamb. God chose from the poorer class to bring forth the King of kings and Lord of lords.

If it was good enough for God's son to be born in a barn, why do we think that we cannot afford children? We needn't own our own home nor have all the modern conveniences before we are ready to have a baby. We don't have to be in the "wealthy class." All we need is willing and welcome hearts. God will always provide for the children He sends.

The poor who have children are richer than the wealthy who reject children.

TRIED AND PROVEN

Matthew Henry said, "He that sends mouths will send meat if we trust in Him."

Dr. Guthrie, who had eleven children, said, "I am rich in nothing but children."

Someone once said to Rev. Moses Browne, who had twelve children, "Sir, you have as many children as Jacob." He replied, "Yes, and I have Jacob's God to provide for them."

QUESTIONS

1. Read Matthew 6:11,28-34 and Philippians 4:19. What are the things that we can expect God to provide for us?

    _____

    _____

    _____

2. Read Proverbs 30:8.

    a. What do you think are the basic necessities for life?

    _____

    _____

    _____

b. Name some of the things that we have in our homes that are unnecessary for basic living and that we could do without if we had to.

_____

_____

_____

3. Statistics reveal that American homes average more televisions per household than children. Share what you think has caused the changing attitude toward children in Western families.

_____

_____

_____

4. How often does God want us to trust Him? Read Psalm 62:8.

_____

_____

_____

5. List the blessings that God has promised to us when we put our total trust in Him, rather than in man's devices or ourselves.

    a. Psalm 18:30; Proverbs 30:5.
        God will be a _____ to us.

    b. Psalm 2:12; 34:8; 84:12; Jeremiah 17:7.
        We will be _____.

    c. Psalm 28:7; 37:40.
        We will be _____.

    d. Psalm 31:19-20a.
        He will hide us _____.

    e. Psalm 31:19-20b.
        He will keep us from _____.

    f. Psalm 32:10.
        We will be surrounded with _____.

    g. Psalm 33:21.
        We shall _____.

    h. Psalm 34:22.
        We will not be _____.

    i. Psalm 36:7-8. We will be abundantly _____.

j. Psalm 37:3. We will be _____.

k. Psalm 56:4,11; Isaiah 12:2.
    We will not be _____.

l. Psalm 125:1.
    We will be _____.

m. Proverbs 16:20.
    We will be _____.

n. Proverbs 28:25.
    We will _____.

o. Proverbs 29:25.
    We will dwell in _____.

p. Isaiah 26:3-4.
    We will have _____.

q. Isaiah 57:13.
    We will _____.

r. Nahum 1:7.
    We will be _____.

s. Jeremiah 17:7-8.
    We will be like _____.

$\mathcal{T}$HE BLESSED SEED

The Same Word

When does life begin? The argument still continues in the world today, but the Word of God is very clear on this subject.

New Testament:

We will look at the New Testament first. The Greek word for "child" is *brephos*. This word is used interchangeably for an "unborn child," a "newborn child," and an "older infant." Consider the following passages:

Luke 1:41-44, "When Elizabeth heard the salutation of Mary, the babe [*brephos*] leaped in her womb; and Elizabeth was filled with the Holy Ghost." This is talking about an unborn child.

Luke 2:12,16, "Ye shall find the babe [*brephos*] in swaddling clothes, lying in a manger." Here the baby has been born, but the same word is used as in the case of the unborn child.

Luke 18:15, "And they brought unto him also infants [*brephos*] that he would touch them...." This passage specifically refers to older babies.

Brephos means "to feed, to nourish." Babies are to be nourished in the womb and when they are born. So we can see that God sees no difference between a baby in the womb and a baby that is born.

Old Testament:

The beauty of Scripture is its unity. So we should not be surprised to discover that the Old Testament reveals the very same perspective on children in and out of the womb, as does the New Testament. Yes, once again God uses the same word for a child that is in the womb as He does for a baby that is outside the womb. Examples are found in Job 3:16 and 1 Samuel 15:3 where the Hebrew word *olal* is used.

Of great significance is the fact that the life which begins at conception, finds its origin and source in the seed of the man (semen), a seed which God declares to be sacred. Contrary to the modern view, which reduces semen to mere bodily fluid, the Bible clearly identifies this as a life-source of tremendous value.

In the case of Onan, he understood that the seed of man was of tremendous value, being inextricably linked with promised generations. The concept of a man's seed within his loins, and a man's seed in the form of living children with souls, was clear. Like many Christians today, Onan wanted the physical union, but he did not want it to result in offspring, so he sought to waste the sperm.

Genesis 38:9, "And Onan knew that the seed [zerah] should not be his; and it came to pass, when he went in unto his brother's wife, that he spilled it on the ground...."

In the levitical law, seed [zerah] is clearly referring to the spilling of semen.

Leviticus 15:16, "If any man's seed of copulation [zerah] go out from him, then he shall wash all his flesh in water...."

In the above Scriptures, zerah is talking about the sperm But in many other Scriptures, God uses this same word zerah to speak of children that are born. There are many Scriptures, but I will just give a few to show the comparison:

Genesis 46:4-6, "Jacob... came to Egypt and all his seed [zerah] with him. His sons and his sons' sons with him, his daughters and his son's daughters, and all his seed [zerah] brought he with him into Egypt."

Psalm 37:25, "I have been young, and now am old; yet have I not seen the righteous forsaken, nor his seed [zerah] begging bread."

Psalm 112:1-2, "Blessed is the man that feareth the Lord, that delighteth greatly in His commandments. His seed [zerah] shall be mighty upon earth."

God makes it very clear that zerah not only means the sperm, but can refer to our living sons and daughters. The sperm is precious to God for it is the life-source of future human beings. Of course, sperm is not soulish, will not live for all eternity, and is not equivalent in value to a human being, but it is clearly a life-source that God links to our progeny and declares to be precious.

In fact, the Bible makes it clear that the entire process of life, from God's design in eternity past, through the act of conception in which an egg is fertilized by sperm, to the preparation of that new life in the womb, to the birth and ultimate ministry of the "seed," is holy, because it is ordained and orchestrated by God, down to the smallest detail.

Note below that God knew Jeremiah before he was even formed. God knows our future children before they are born. He is totally sovereign and in control of the glorious process of life, every step of which is precious to him.

Jeremiah 1:5, "*Before* I formed thee in the womb I knew thee; and *before* thou camest forth out of the womb I sanctified thee, and I ordained thee a prophet unto the nations."

Psalm 139:16 (NIV), "Your eyes saw my unformed body. *All* the days ordained for me were written in your book *before* one of them came to be."

In fact, God speaks of these children as having resided in the very loins of their great, grandfathers:

Hebrews 7:9-10, "Levi, also, who received tithes, paid tithes in Abraham. For *he was yet in the loins of his father* when Melchizedek met him."

Commenting on the above passage, author George Henderson notes that: "Levi embryonically paid tithes in his great grandfather Abraham, and Melchizedek collected them." Barclay's version says, "Levi... was in his father's body when Melchizedek met him."

Abraham was Levi's great grandfather. Levi was not even a twinkle in his eye when he met Melchizedek, but God says (not man, but God) that he was actually in the loins of Abraham, even though he was not yet born! He actually paid tithes in Abraham, even though he was not yet thought of by man. This is "God-thinking", not "man-thinking!" No wonder it says in Proverbs 23:22, "Hearken unto thy father that begat thee."

Some Bible commentators say that Job 10:10-11 explains conception and gestation. "Hast thou not poured me out as milk [the sperm travelling to the womb] and curdled me like cheese [conception]? Thou hast clothed me with skin and flesh, and hast knit me together with bones and sinews [implantation and formation]." Even though he was only a sperm, notice that Job says, "poured *me* out" and "curdled *me*." Note that Job considered himself as much a person when he was growing in the womb as when he wrote those words.

Now we can understand why God viewed Onan's attempt to deliberately thwart conception as wicked and worthy of capital punishment. He participated in intercourse but thwarted the natural process of conception. His act was the spilling of seed which was given to him by God for a specific purpose (the conception of life) and a perversion of the unity of love and life which God has decreed would be part of the act of intimacy between a man and a woman.

God's judgment on Onan was death. How grateful I am for God's mercy on this generation. But how long can we be complacent knowing that, absent a change of heart, we as a people will someday be held accountable for our many anti-family, anti-life philosophies and deeds?

When Onan spilled the seed on the ground, he was self-consciously trying to prevent his seed from becoming a human being. God's plan was that Onan would be in the lineage of the Messiah, a privilege that was taken from Onan and passed to Judah. Commenting on the Scriptural account of Onan, John Calvin takes the bold and unequivocal stand about the sacredness of sperm as a life-force when he writes: "For this is to extinguish the hope of the race and to kill before he is born the hoped-for offspring."

There is much debate over the incident of Onan. Some would reduce the sin of Onan to the fact that he did not want to contribute to his brother's lineage. This is clearly part of the issue, but the context indicates that more than a bad attitude was involved in Onan's sin. Onan was punished for his actions: He deliberately tried to thwart God's process of procreation so that there would be no offspring. Onan would not have been executed had he simply refused to take to wife his deceased brother's former spouse. The death penalty is not a biblical remedy for refusing to play the part of a kinsman redeemer, but it was the penalty God chose for Onan's moral perversion, which is ultimately the crime of which Onan was guilty when he deliberately sought to separate life from love and reduce intimacy to a sexual act where the sperm is treated without respect, and the God-ordained, natural functions of the human body are not honored.

It is difficult to appreciate God's hatred for the sin of Onan, when we live in a culture that has reduced the beauty of sexual intimacy to a selfish quest for personal pleasure. It is even more difficult when we realize that most of the Church has adopted the world's attitude toward life and love. However, rather than making excuses for the sins of this generation, would it not be a better approach to confess our own guilt in the sin of Onan, and to seek God afresh? He promises forgiveness to all who seek him.

God forbid that any of us pervert the natural functions of the bodies God has given to us, so as to free us from offspring. God forbid that we would miss out on the blessing of future generations because of our own selfishness.

QUESTIONS

1. In the light of the above truth, what should we do about contraceptive methods that destroy the sperm?

    _____

    _____

    _____

2. We have learned that God uses the same word for a child in the womb as a child that is born. How does this revelation affect your actions?

    _____

    _____

    _____

3. Read Psalm 139:16, Jeremiah 1:5, and Hebrews 7:9-10 again. God says that He knows us before we are born. How does this relate to contraception?

_____

_____

_____

4. Explain how God sees children in the light of Hebrews 7: 9-10.

_____

_____

_____

CHAPTER 11

*W*HEN DID CONTRACEPTION BEGIN?

It is hard to believe that we, the people of God who confess that we believe in His truth, have embraced a deceptive philosophy that was born in sin and seduction. The birth control movement was heralded and made public by Margaret Sanger, a woman who ferociously believed in Malthusian Eugenics and who practiced and promoted blatant sexual promiscuity. Margaret Sanger championed the cause of the elimination of inferior races. Her plan was to "create a race of thoroughbreds." She coined names for all those who were not of the superior Aryan race—"morons, misfits, and the maladjusted" and "defectives, delinquents, and dependents." She believed that the physically unfit, the materially poor, the racially inferior—including the Jews and the African Americans—must be restricted or eliminated. Contraception, sterilization, and abortion were the perfect methods for getting rid of these "human weeds."

This is the origin of today's birth control movement which the Christian church has ignorantly embraced.

Margaret's Sanger's first paper was called *The Woman Rebel*. The first issue denounced marriage as "a degenerate institution" and sexual modesty as "obscene prudery." She fought against the "smothering restrictions of marital fidelity." She later edited *The Birth Control Review* and unfortunately by 1922 her name had become a household word. She continued to fervently champion for sexual freedom and its sisters— birth control, sterilization, and abortion. She organized the Birth Control League, the foundation for the later worldwide Planned Parenthood, now part of our society. Her ardency to sterilize the "choking human undergrowth" of "morons and imbeciles" has reached every strata of society. It is now accepted without argument by non-Christian and Christian alike. Isn't it amazing that as something becomes part of society, we accept it without question? This is dangerous.

WE CANNOT BE NEUTRAL

God's people are exhorted to "abhor that which is evil," but instead we have embraced this evil. We have done it without consciously realizing it. We gradually succumbed to the philosophy of the world until this philosophy has now become a belief in the church. Isn't it amazing how the spirit of the world can conform us to its thinking? As God-fearing people, we must constantly challenge our beliefs to make sure they are not the world's thinking, but that they line up with God's Word. We cannot be neutral. If we don't take a strong stand against evil, we will gradually gravitate toward it, and in time, it will become part of our lives. Psalm 106: 34-35 (TMB) says, "They did not wipe out those godless cultures as ordered by God; instead they intermarried with the heathen, and in time became just like them."

When we accept and "live out" Margaret Sanger's plan of "contraception, sterilization, and abortion," we change sides and fight for the evil one. Margaret Sanger says, "Birth control appeals to the advanced radical because it is calculated to undermine the authority of the Christian churches. I look forward to seeing humanity free someday of the tyranny of Christianity no less than Capitalism." Elsewhere Sanger said, "The most educational approach to the Negro is through a religious appeal. We do not want word to go out that we want to exterminate the Negro population, and the Minister is the man who can straighten out that idea if it ever occurs to any of their more rebellious members."

Notice dear reader, that the words, "contraception, sterilization, and abortion" are always used together. They are a threesome in feminist and humanist literature. They use these three weapons for the same purpose—to eliminate children! As Christians, we have tried to separate contraception and sterilization from the issue of abortion. But they all have the same purpose. In fact, abortion is a back-up plan to eliminate life if contraception and sterilization are not successful.

It is interesting that Satan, who comes with his three-pronged attack to "steal, kill, and destroy," exposes his "elimination life program" with another threesome of "contraception, sterilization, and abortion." Each one is masterminded in hell!

We mourn the death of forty-three millions babies who have been aborted since *Roe* v. *Wade*. We cry out to God for this to be reversed. However, I do not think that we will see a victory in stopping abortion until God's people repent over their attitude toward children. While we carry this negative attitude toward "life" and toward receiving children from God, we will see no change. It is time for us to awake out of our sleep and realize whose kingdom we are following. It is time for us to see "life" the way God sees it. It is time for us to repent.

Contraception was not entertained by the Christian church—Protestant or Catholic—until as late as 1930. Until this time, it was considered by church theologians to be the "murder of future unborn children." But slowly, the campaigning of Margaret Sanger and her cohorts began to infiltrate the church. So how did it come to be accepted by the church today?

The following historical facts are quoted and used by permission from *Birth Control and Christian Discipleship* by John F. Kippley. Available from The Couple to Couple League, P.O. Box 111184, Cincinnati, OH 45211-1184, www.ccli.org.

THE LAMBETH CONFERENCES OF 1908 AND 1920

The Church of England at its Lambeth Conference of bishops in 1908 discussed and repudiated the practice of contraception. At its 1920 Lambeth Conference, the Anglican Church fathers acknowledged the contraception debate but responded, "We urge the paramount importance in married life of deliberate and thoughtful self-control...." In Resolution 68 of the 1920 Conference, they added, "We utter an emphatic warning against the use of unnatural means for the avoidance of conception."

THE ANGLICAN BREAK: 1930

Thus, it is apparent that in the nineteenth century and the early part of the twentieth century, the conviction of Protestant leadership was that unnatural means of birth control were immoral, and this was likewise the constant teaching of the Catholic Church. Despite the fact that reduced birth rates and contraceptive propaganda were making it evident that some or many church members were not living up to the moral teachings, the teaching of the churches had not changed. The beginning of 1930 still saw moral unanimity among Christian churches that unnatural means of birth control were morally wrong, incompatible with a life of Christian discipleship.

However, in 1930 a revolution occurred. On August 14, during the Lambeth Conference of 1930, the assembled Anglican bishops broke with the previously unanimous Christian doctrine and allowed unnatural birth control devices and practices. Their statement in Resolution 15 is worth repeating since it is historic:

Where there is a clearly felt moral obligation to limit or avoid parenthood, the method must be decided on Christian principles. The primary and obvious method is complete abstinence from intercourse (as far as may be necessary) in a life of discipleship and self-control lived in the power of the Holy Spirit. Nevertheless in those cases where there is such a clearly felt moral obligation to limit or avoid parenthood, and where there is a morally sound reason for avoiding complete abstinence, the Conference agrees that other methods may be used, provided that this is done in the light of the same Christian principles. The Conference records its strong condemnation of the use of any methods of conception-control from motives of selfishness, luxury, or mere convenience.

The Conference, which passed Resolution 15 with a vote of 193 to 67 (46 not voting) also recognized that up until that time the Anglican church had taught "that the use of preventive methods is in all cases unlawful for a Christian."

Within a few months, the Anglican break was echoed in the United States. In March of 1931, the majority of a committee of the Federal Council of Churches, a forerunner of today's National Council of Churches, endorsed "the careful and restrained use of contraceptives by married people," at the same time admitting that "serious evils, such as extramarital sex relations, may be increased by general knowledge of contraceptives."

The reaction was immediate and provides a good reflection of that day's leadership opinion. The earliest dated comment in my possession comes from an editorial in the *Washington Post*, March 22, 1931:

> Carried to its logical conclusion, the committee's report, if carried into effect, would wound the death-knell of marriage as a holy institution by establishing degrading practices which would encourage indiscriminate immorality. The suggestion that the use of legalized contraceptives would be "careful and restrained" is preposterous.

Strong criticism followed in Protestant church monthlies and from leading spokesmen:

> Birth control, as popularly understood today and involving the use of contraceptives, is one of the most repugnant of modern aberrations, representing a 20th century renewal of pagan bankruptcy. (Dr. Walter A. Maier)

> It is of prime significance that the present agitation for birth control occurs at a period which is notorious for looseness in sexual morality. This fact creates suspicion as to the motives for the agitation, and should warn true-minded men and women against the surrender of themselves as tools for unholy purposes. (Dr. F. H. Knubel, President, United Lutheran Churches)

FROM CONTRACEPTION TO ABORTION

The groundwork for unlimited abortion was laid through the "logic" of the acceptance of contraception. The first step was taken at the 1930 Lambeth Conference, which stated that the birth control method "must be decided on Christian principles." The final step was taken by the very next sentence in that same NCC statement which is tragic in its irony. "Protestant Christians are agreed in condemning abortion or any method which destroys human life except when the health or life of the mother is at stake." I call this a tragic irony because that statement, which on the face of it appears to be anti-abortion, is in reality the basis for most of the millions upon millions of abortions that occur each year in the Free World. The most common reason given for abortion is typically the "mental health" of the mother, a term broad enough to cover anything from schizophrenia to a headache.

Among Protestant Churches represented by the Church of England and those in the National Council of Churches, it took thirty-one years to go from the acceptance of contraception in 1930 to accepting abortion for the health of the mother in 1961. In the American legal system, it took thirty-seven years from an 1836 court decision permitting doctors to import contraceptives to the 1973 abortion decision allowing doctors to kill unborn babies. In 1984, a Planned Parenthood abortion facility listed fifty-two North American churches and church organizations as supporting the right to choose abortion as a method of birth control.

QUESTIONS

From the early 1900s, our forefathers and foremothers have gradually imbibed the humanistic philosophies of the unbelievers. These attitudes have been passed on to us from generation to generation and now we think they are the truth.

1. What can we do to halt this pattern and save the coming generation from continuing in this trend?

    _____

    _____

    _____

2. How can we discern the deceptive philosophies of the world? How can we tell what is "the world" and what is "from God?"

    _____

    _____

    _____

3. Why does the church, which is "the pillar and ground of truth," conform so easily to the standards of the world?

_____

_____

_____

To WHICH KINGDOM DO YOU BELONG?

I have just received another telephone call, one of many that I constantly receive week by week every year. A mother tells me the great news that she is having another baby. She wants someone to rejoice with her, but she is too scared to tell her parents or in-laws. They are likely to throw a fit!

Why is there such an aversion to the prospect of life? Of course, once the little baby comes, the grandparents will love the baby. Who can resist a sweet baby? But why do they, and all the other ill-wishers, put up every opposition at the contemplation of the child being born? Why have we assimilated the anti-child philosophy of this world? Why have we fallen into the plans of the enemy who hates life? Are we so easily squeezed into the mold of this world?

I can expect this attitude from those who don't acknowledge God, but it causes my heart to ache when I find it is the attitude of those who own the name of the Lord. Some weeks ago I spoke at a home schooling meeting, and in the course of my message I asked the question, "Hands up those who have a new life in their womb?" To my amazement, no hands went up! And this was amongst about sixty women of childbearing age!

How can this attitude be on the lips of those who preach on the behalf of the God who loves children? Last year a mother came to an *Above Rubies* retreat in Wisconsin. She had been convicted for about four years to get a reversal from her tubal ligation, but was waiting for her husband's consent. At the retreat she purchased a book called *A Change of Heart* (fifty testimonies of couples who have had reversals), which she took home to her husband. God touched his heart, too. They shared their desire with their pastor who was so antagonistic that he put them out of the church!

GOD GIVES LIFE, THE DEVIL SNUFFS IT OUT!

God's kingdom is a kingdom of life. He is the author of life. He is the one who breathes life into every human being. He loves life. Because He is the author of life, it is precious to Him. Do we value life the same way that God does? Let's look at the Scriptures for further understanding.

Genesis 2:7, "And the Lord God formed man of the dust of the ground, and breathed into his nostrils the breath of life; and man became a living soul."

Job 12:10, "In whose hand is the soul of every living thing, and the breath of all mankind."

Job 33:4, "The Spirit of God has made me, and the breath of the Almighty has given me life."

Isaiah 42:5, "Thus saith God the Lord… He that gives breath unto the people upon it, and spirit to them that walk therein."

Zechariah 12:1, "The Lord… that forms the spirit of man within him."

Acts 17:25, "He gives to all life, and breath."

John 10:10 (RSV), "The thief comes only to steal and kill and destroy; I came that they may have life, and have it abundantly."

At every strategic time of history, Satan has tried to eliminate life. At the time that God was preparing a nation to show His light to the world, Satan tried to kill all the baby boys, but Moses was miraculously spared. When the time came for God to bring His holy Son into the world, Satan once again tried to kill all the babies, but Jesus was sovereignly spared. Now at this time when God is looking for a people to fulfill His purposes like no other time in history, Satan is once again trying to eliminate the army of God. Over these last few decades, he has been very successful. Born-again, God-loving Christians have fallen into His deceptive plan and helped him reduce God's army. How long will we continue to become his pawns?

GOD'S KINGDOM IS LIFE, SATAN'S KINGDOM LEADS TO DESTRUCTION

Jesus said in Mark 10:13-15 (TMB), "Don't push these children away. Don't ever get between them and Me. These children are at the very center of life in the kingdom." Children are at the heart of God's kingdom.

Jesus is the Prince of Life (Acts 3:15) whereas Satan is the prince of this world which is governed by the power of darkness and death.

GOD'S WAY LEADS TO LIFE, SATAN'S WAY LEADS TO DESTRUCTION

Matthew 7:13-14 (RSV), "Enter by the narrow gate; for the gate is wide and the way is easy, that leads to destruction, and those who enter by it are many. For the gate is narrow and the way is hard, that leads to life, and those who find it are few."

The way to life is not the easy way. It is not popular to embrace life. It is the narrow way that not many choose, but it is the way of blessing.

MOTHER—YOU ARE A LIFE-GIVER!

Dear precious mother, don't despise the gift that God has given you. You have been ordained to nurture and bring forth life. You are a life-giver. This is the most awesome privilege in the whole of the world. Contemplate it! Not only do you have the honor of bringing a life into the world, but a soul that will live forever. When a new baby is conceived in your womb, you have eternity in your womb. You bring forth a life that will last forever and ever. Motherhood is an eternal career. It carries on into the eons of eternity. One of the greatest deceptions of Satan is to seduce mothers to be captivated with their careers and ministry outside the home so they don't have time to create life. All their material "things" will be left behind. Instead, they will be empty of that which they could have taken into eternity—the redeemed souls of their children.

The enemy knows the power of life. Every human being that comes into the world is another potential for God's purposes and glory and to destroy the works of the enemy. This is why Satan tries to destroy God's purpose for mothers. The greatest threat to him is a mother who understands her calling, to nurture and nourish life, to train, polish, and sharpen these children for God's mighty purposes—and for the eternal age.

Psalm 104:30 says, "You send forth your Spirit, they are created; and you renew the face of the earth." Each new baby renews the face of the earth. Each new life that is conceived is an opportunity for God to wondrously move and show forth His power. Every child? Yes, even children from impossible beginnings have often risen to greatness. I think of Jephthah who was one of the leaders of Israel. He was born of a prostitute. He was thrust out of his father's house and refused any inheritance. Yet with all these setbacks, he became a great warrior and a judge of Israel!

S.D. Gordon, in *Quiet Talks on Home Ideals*, writes of the new baby. "The new-born babe is a fresh act of God. He is the latest revelation of God's creative handiwork.... The babe is a marvel of possibility! The man who will sway thousands to his will as the whirlwind sweeps the forest, lies sleeping in that babe. The organizer of the world's industries, or the leader of the world's thought, or the changer of the world's life, and of the map of the earth, is in that wee morsel of humanity lying in his mother's arms. That cooing voice may compel the whole world to listen. Those fat dainty fingers may pen words that a world will be eager to read. A Wesley or a Faraday may be there, only waiting the coming of his day of action. And, far more than these, the man who will re-live Jesus' life, with all its simplicity and purity and fragrance, in some humble corner, that will touch and tinge deeply the life of the crowd, may lie there all open to the impress of father and mother."

THE TIME OF LIFE

The Bible calls pregnancy and birthing *"the time of life."*

Read the story of Sarah in Genesis 18:10-14, "I will certainly return unto thee according to *the time of life*; and, lo, Sarah thy wife shall have a son."

Read the story of the Shunamite woman in 2 Kings 4:12-17, "About this season, according to *the time of life*, thou shalt embrace a son."

WHICH WILL YOU CHOOSE?

As God put the challenge before the Israelites in Moses' day, He lays it before us again today. He waits for us to choose.

Deuteronomy 30:15-16, "See, I have set before you today life and good, death and evil, in that I command you today to love the Lord your God, to walk in His ways, and to keep His commandments, His statutes and His judgments, that you may live and multiply; and the Lord your God will bless you in the land which you go to possess.... I call heaven and earth as witnesses today against you, that I have set before you life and death, blessing and cursing: therefore choose life, that both you and your descendants may live...."

God makes things plain for us to understand. He doesn't beat around the bush. God calls life good. He calls it a blessing. And we had better not contradict God. In Isaiah 5:20, He says, "Woe to those who call evil good, and good evil; who put darkness for light, and light for darkness; who put bitter for sweet, and sweet for bitter!"

Which will you choose?

QUESTIONS

1. Read Proverbs 19:23. What will we choose if we walk in the fear of the Lord?

    _____

    _____

    _____

2. Read Ezekiel 33:15 and John 6:63. What are God's statutes called?

    _____

    _____

    _____

3. Read Genesis 9:5. What does God require at the hand of every man?

    _____

    _____

    _____

4. Why do you think many people have a negative attitude toward life in the womb and yet embrace life when it is born?

    _____

    _____

    _____

5. Share or write how you feel Mary felt when she said the words in Luke 1:38, "Behold the handmaid of the Lord; be it unto me according to thy word."

    _____

    _____

    _____

6. Read Genesis 30:1-2. How do we know from this Scripture that it is God who gives conception?

    _____

    _____

    _____

$\mathscr{P}$ROTECT YOUR UNBORN BABIES FROM DEATH

It is very sad, but many God-fearing Christian couples unknowingly abort their own babies. The Pill is a common form of birth control and is used by many Christians. Both the Pill and the IUD can and do act as abortifacients. Unfortunately, doctors do not tell their patients this information. Nor do we hear pastors warning the families in their congregations that they could be aborting their own offspring.

There are two kinds of Pill:

The Combination Pill. It contains artificial estrogen and progesterone. When a woman ovulates, the pituitary gland stimulates her ovaries. The Combination Pill stops this process most of the time. However, studies reveal that about ten percent of the time, there is break-through ovulation allowing conception to take place.

The Mini-pill. This is only progestin based and therefore generally does not suppress ovulation. If it does not suppress ovulation, how does it prevent a baby from being conceived? There is another mechanism that takes place. The progestin in the Combination Pill, and the solely progestin in the Mini-pill, cause the lining of the womb to become thin and shriveled, so when a newly conceived baby tries to implant in the womb, it cannot because the endometrium is shriveled up. What happens to his new little life? It dies. Abortion takes place.

Dear husbands and wives, please realize that there is the possibility of conception ten percent of the time with the Combination Pill and the majority of the time with the Mini-pill. Although this is against everything in your heart, if you have been using the Pill, you may have unknowingly aborted your own babies.

It is important to confess this sin and repent of it before the Lord. Jesus died, not only for your deliberate sins, but also for your sins of ignorance. Hebrews 9:7 says, "But into the second went the high priest alone once every year, not without blood, which he offered for himself, and for the errors [*agnoema*] of the people." This Greek word means "the sins of ignorance and thoughtlessness." Read also Numbers 15:28.

I now quote from John Kippley in *Birth Control and Christian Discipleship*. Available from The Couple to Couple League, P.O. Box 11184, Cincinnati, OH 45211-1184, www.ccli.org.

In all probability, more newly-conceived humans beings are destroyed each year by the intrauterine device (IUD) and the Pill than by surgical abortions. An "abortifacient" is a device or drug that causes an abortion. There is no question that both the IUD and the Pill can and do achieve their birth control effectiveness at times by causing very early abortions. In 1989, Mr. Frank Sussman, an attorney for Missouri abortion clinics, argued before the U.S. Supreme Court that "IUDs [and] low-dose birth control pills... act as abortifacients."

A 1984 pro-Pill pamphlet from the Federal government notes that, "though rare, it is possible for women using combined pills (synthetic estrogen and progestogen) to ovulate. Then other mechanisms work to prevent pregnancy. Both kinds of pills make the cervical mucus thick and 'inhospitable' to sperm, discouraging any entry to the uterus. In addition, they make it difficult for a fertilized egg to implant, causing changes in fallopian tube contractions and in the uterine lining. These actions explain why the mini pill works, as it generally does not suppress ovulation."

From my personal study of pregnancy charts, I am not at all impressed by the ability of thickened cervical mucus to prevent sperm migration into the uterus. This observation has been confirmed by a multi-national study indicating that the days of 'sticky' mucus or thick mucus near ovulation are just as fertile as the days of the most fertile type of mucus near ovulation. Thus, resistance to sperm migration does not appear to be a significant factor in the birth control effectiveness of the Pill.

While it is impossible to estimate precisely the number of early abortions caused by the IUD and the Pill, enough is known to illustrate the magnitude of this evil. The only real question is about how often these devices and drugs act as abortifacients and how many early abortions they cause.

The IUD is largely off the market in the United States because of massive lawsuits for damages suffered by American women, but it is still widely used in Third World countries whose women do not have access to the courts for similar damages. It has been generally recognized since the early 1970s that the primary action of the IUD is to prevent implantation of the week-old new human life in its embryo stage or development: pro-abortion organizations have used full-page ads to warn that a Human Life Amendment to protect human babies from the moment of conception would outlaw both the IUD and the Pill.

In the United States in 1988, there were still over one million women using the IUD, and they cause perhaps almost three million micro-abortions each year. (See "The Arithmetic of Abortifacient Birth Control" below.

On a worldwide basis, the figures are simply mind-boggling. A London physician, trying to justify "test tube babies" and frozen embryos, said that if people were really concerned about early human life, "they wouldn't use the IUD which destroys fifty million embryos each month around the world." That would yield the terrifying figure of six hundred million early abortions each year on a worldwide basis. I think Dr. Winston was assuming over an eighty percent pregnancy rate each month, and that's probably high. The twenty-five percent rate I have used in the abortifacient arithmetic box yields the still-terrifying figure of 247 million early abortions each year, based on the estimate of eighty-four million IUD users throughout the world, including fifty million in China.

The Pill may cause more early abortions in the United States than are caused by chemical and surgical abortions. With an estimated 13.8 million American women on the Pill, they may well be causing approximately two million early abortions each year.

In short, the death toll from the IUD and the Pill exceeds that of the Nazi Holocaust—each year—in the United States alone. What that means is that even apart from surgical abortion, the methods of birth control used by millions of people who call themselves Christians are destroying millions of human lives each year. Add to these figures the early abortions from IUDs and Pills used worldwide by non-Christians; then add the fifty million surgical/chemical later abortions each year, what you now have are numbers that every two or three years vastly exceed the 250 to 300 million deaths estimated to result from a major power nuclear war. It is no small wonder that an increasing number of people are saying that we have richly earned such a holocaust and marvel at God's forbearance in the face of such worldwide contempt for His gift of life.

If the Christian churches had remained firm in their rejection of unnatural methods of birth control, would any of this be taking place? If they had remained firm, I believe there is utterly no question that the present abortion holocaust would only be a fraction of its present magnitude.

THE ARITHMETIC OF ABORTIFACIENT BIRTH CONTROL

Unobstructed intercourse at the fertile time does not always result in pregnancy. However, the probability of conception occurring for a couple not using anti-conception devices (condom, diaphragm, and spermicides) is at least twenty-five percent in any given cycle among normally fertile couples of average sexual activity, and it ranges up to sixty-eight percent for couples who have relations every day during the fertile time. The lower figure of twenty-five percent will be used in describing the magnitude of early abortions with the IUD and the Pill; it is conservative relative to the coital patterns stated by Kinsey for American couples where wives are under forty. Thus, a pregnancy rate of .25 in each cycle among one million women using IUDs every cycle would result in 250,000 conceptions per month. An average of twelve menstrual-fertility cycles per year would yield three million IUD-caused early abortions. However, since the IUD has about a five percent surprise pregnancy rate, among one million IUD users in the U.S. there would be approximately fifty-thousand recognized pregnancies each year, many to be killed later by surgical abortion. Subtracting these 50,000 from the directly IUD-caused abortions yields an estimated 2.95 million early abortions each year caused by the IUD. Multiply that by eighty-four for the estimate of the world total—247.8 million early abortions each year.

Estimates about the number of abortions caused by the Pill are more difficult because of the triple-threat action of the Pill. The older high dosage pills had "breakthrough ovulation" rates of between two percent and ten percent. Given the lower dosage in today's Pills and the numbers of women using the Mini-pill which apparently has almost no suppression of ovulation, the ten percent figure does not seem unreasonable to use, but we can calculate it both ways. Among the 13.8 million American women using the Pill, the ten percent rate would yield 1.38 million ovulatory cycles each month. Applying the twenty-five percent overall conception rate would yield 345,000 conceptions each month or 4.14 million new lives each year, almost all of which would be aborted by the implantation-resisting effects of the Pill.

A 4.7% rate of breakthrough ovulation was observed and reported in 1984. Applying that rate to the 13.8 million American women on the Pill would yield 648,600 ovulations and an estimated 162,150 new lives conceived each cycle, or 1,945,800 each year, almost all of whom would be denied implantation and thus aborted. Again, such figures are only for the United States and would need to be multiplied by 4.3 times for the rest of the world.

Recommended Reading: For further information regarding the aborttifacient implications of the Pill, I recommend *Does the Birth Control Pill Cause Abortions?* by Randy Alcorn, currently in its fifth revised edition and published by Eternal Perspective Ministries, Gresham, Oregon. It can be downloaded from www.epm.org/bcpill.pdf.

QUESTIONS

1. What should we do about informing couples of the
    dangers of the Pill and the IUD? Should we allow them
    to continue in ignorance when there is the possibility
    that they are aborting their own children?

    _____

    _____

    _____

2. Can you think of some of the reasons why a mother
    would choose abortion?

    _____

    _____

    _____

3. What are some of the reasons why couples choose to use contraception?

_____

_____

_____

4. Look at your answers for numbers two and three and state how the reasons for abortion and contraception are closely linked.

_____

_____

_____

CHAPTER 14

THE SOVEREIGNTY OF GOD

W e are familiar with the phrase, "If He is not Lord of all, He is not Lord at all."

These words apply to every part of our lives, which includes our fertility.

Many of us sing the beautiful song, "Sovereign, Lord, reign in me…." We mean it with all our hearts, but sadly, our minds are still conditioned by humanistic thinking. If we are honest, we must confess that we do not allow God to have control over our reproduction. Even though He is the one who designed and created the womb, we do not want Him to have any control over it. We do not even want it to function the way that God has planned.

Although God is sovereign, we do not allow Him to be sovereign in our lives. Many would find it easier to yield themselves to go to the mission field than to yield their womb to the Lord.

A friend of mine is in the process of writing an article on this subject, and she is naming it, "I surrender *almost* all." I think this is a very correct title. Can we truly sing with truthfulness the wonderful old hymn, "I surrender all," or would we have to say, "I surrender almost all?" Many would have to say these words, "Lord, I surrender my life to you, all except my womb. I have to have control over this."

YIELD EACH MEMBER OF YOUR BODY TO THE LORD

Romans 6:13, "Neither yield ye your members as instruments of unrighteousness unto sin: but yield yourselves unto God, as those that are alive from the dead, and your members as instruments of righteousness unto God."

Romans 12:1, "I beseech you therefore, brethren, by the mercies of God, that ye present your bodies a living sacrifice, holy [*devoted, consecrated*], acceptable unto God, which is your reasonable [*rational, intelligent*] service." Here we are exhorted to present every member of our body to the Lord. Would this not also include our reproductive organs?

1 Corinthians 6:19-20, "What, know ye not that your body is the temple of the Holy Ghost which is in you, which ye have of God, and ye are not your own? For ye are bought with a price: therefore glorify God in your body, and in your spirit, which are God's."

Notice that God's Word says that not only our soul and our spirit, but that our body is the temple of the Holy Spirit. God wants us to glorify Him in our bodies, too. The word "glorify" is the Greek word *doxazo* which means "to recognize, to honor." If we are to glorify God in our body, as the Scripture invokes, we are to recognize and honor His Lordship over our body, which includes our reproduction.

Every member of our body is needed. The medical profession has taken out spleens, tonsils, adenoids, and so on—saying they were unnecessary. However, modern research has proved that these organs are important to the body. Every member of the body has its importance in relation to other members of the body. The Word says that, "when one members suffers, all members suffer with it" (1 Corinthians 12:20-24). God's Word is eternally true. If we cut out or destroy one member of the body, other members of the body will suffer. We cannot get away from the perfect way that God designed our bodies.

Research has now shown that the root cause of many diseases that a lot of men experience today is because they have had a vasectomy. The following are just a few of the diseases that have been observed in vasectomized men:

Thrombophlebitis; pulmonary embolism; infections of the prostate gland, epididymis (a tube leading from the testis), kidney, blood, heart valves, abscess of the liver, abscesses of the skin, recurrent sinusitis, recurrent virus infection; arthritis; narcolepsy; multiple sclerosis; migraine and related headaches; hypoglycemia; allergic manifestations; emotional disturbances; impaired sexual function; kidney stones, angina pectoris and myocardial infarction; tumors and cancer (especially of the prostrate).

Are you concerned about prostrate cancer? Dr. H.J. Roberts cites a study on this disease in his book, *Is Vasectomy Worth the Risk?* "Giovannucci, et al, reported statistically significant increases of prostate cancer in both a large prospective cohort study (1993a) and a large retrospective cohort study (1993b) of vasectomized men in the United States—viz., 10,055 and 14,607 subjects respectively. The overall risk increased by 56 percent but rose up to 89 percent among those who had undergone vasectomy 22 years or longer. Such risk did not appear to be related to diet, level of physical activity, smoking, alcohol intake, educational level, body mass index, geographical area or residence, or detection bias in these carefully conceived studies."

Any man contemplating a vasectomy should first read the following books written by Dr. H.J. Roberts who was chosen as the Best Doctor in the U.S. and was selected for inclusion in Who's Who in America, Who's Who in the World, and Who's Who in Science and Engineering. *Is Vasectomy Worth the Risk? A Physician's Case Against Vasectomania* (Sunshine Sentinel Press, May 1993). *Is Vasectomy Safe? Medical Risks and Legal Implications* (Sunshine Sentinel Press, May 1993).

What about a tubal ligation? Even this surgery is not without risk. Dr. Vicki Hufnagel, the pioneer in female reconstructive surgery who wrote *No More Hysterectomies*, states:

My clinical observations have been born out by scientific investigations. Many studies confirm the existence of post-tubal ligation syndrome and show that existing menstrual problems can be aggravated by tubal sterilization. Three theories explain why these problems occur:

1. Tubal ligation destroys the blood supply to the ovaries.

2. Certain types of tubal sterilization procedures are more likely to result in endometriosis.

3. An increase in the blood pressure within the ovarian artery can create an estrogen-progesterone imbalance.

Many studies confirm finding varicosities (abnormal swelling or enlargements) in ovarian veins, hormonal imbalances, and fistulas of the fallopian tubes, which are associated with endometriosis in women who have been sterilized.

The most frequent type of sterilization in the 1970s involved burning the tubes during laparoscopy. Not only does this run the risk of burning the bowels but it creates massive tissue damage and adhesions. If a patient of mine chooses to have her tubes tied, I prefer clipping the tubes closed, because this method presents few post-operative problems.

I believe that the fallopian tubes need to be open and working. In a tubal ligation, we burn or clip them closed. If retrograde or backup bleeding occurs during menstruation the tubes blow up and become swollen and inflamed. The ovaries need to be nourished by oxygen and blood.

Probably one of the most serious consequences of post-tubal ligation syndrome is that it may lead to hysterectomy. There is terrible irony in this. Imagine going in to have your tubes tied, thinking that this will finally take care of all your contraception needs, only to discover months later that your cramps are worse, the bleeding more intense. And from your complaints comes the recommendation for hysterectomy. Studies have shown that post-tubal problems worsen with time.

Can we allow God to be God in our lives? Can we truly let Him be Sovereign Lord?

The following testimonies are just a sample of literally thousands of couples who have now regretted their decision to cut off their ability to conceive.

I SURRENDER—ALMOST ALL!

"When I was newly married, I assumed that someone would talk to me about birth control and such matters as 'how many children were enough.' However, I discovered this subject was not open for discussion in the church… at least not with any clear answers. I was left with the impression that it is a personal decision between the husband, wife, and their doctor.

"My mother and father had officially disowned me and I thought that each child I had could possibly bring about the reconciliation I so desired. However, it never happened. After I had two baby boys, twenty-one months apart, I figured that we should go in and get 'fixed.' My husband wasn't totally convinced about the permanent procedure but wanted to please me. I was emotionally exhausted. I decided that I could not handle having one more child. We decided that he should go and have a vasectomy performed. After all, we couldn't afford to feed, clothe, and take care of more than two children. It was the logical thing to do. Besides, we'd never have to worry about birth control again. Just think of the savings! By the way, I was only twenty-one years old!

"My husband had the procedure done and I did not give it a second thought—until two years later. You never think you will make it past the baby stage—loads of laundry, constant physical demands, and mental atrophy—but you do. I did make it through and when I got to the other side a strange thing happened. I missed the baby stage. However, I was content with our decision and had settled into our 'typical' family with ease.

"It was around this time that we went to Nashville, Tennessee to make an album. We left the boys with my husband's family for two weeks and were on our way. I was excited! I had my childbearing out of the way, my figure back in shape, and was now looking forward to a musical career.

"While we were in Nashville working on our recording, I asked the lady of the house (in the home studio) for something good to read. She handed me a copy of *All the Way Home* by Mary Pride. I read through the entire book in one day. I sat there in the hallway on the floor, glued to every word on every page. My eyes filled with tears as I read about what it really means to be a mother. I saw that children were a blessing to be treasured and not just a duty to be done with. I was so seriously convicted about my selfish attitude toward motherhood. I couldn't see through the tears for days. My heart ached with remorse for holding back a part of my life from the Lord. It was is if I had said, 'I surrender almost all!' I had given my life to the Lord, but not totally. I trusted the Lord, but not fully. The conviction was almost more than I could bear. My husband and I prayed together and repented for the decision we'd made.

"We then began investigating reversal doctors—how discouraging. For a procedure that cost $300 to do, undoing it cost $2,500! Ouch! The Lord eventually led us to a doctor in Arkansas and we had the reversal done for a fraction of the cost. It has been two years now since that surgery was performed and we are trusting that God will give us more children if it is His will. I want to surrender all to Him, not almost all."

WE MISSED OUT!

"When we were first married we believed with our hearts that God would give us the children He wanted us to have. We trusted Him for seven years and are ashamed to say that our selfishness took over and we allowed the world to influence us to the point that we cut off children in a sterilization surgery eight years ago. Two years ago we were led to have a reversal surgery done. One year ago our merciful God blessed us with a son."

A CHANGE OF CONVICTIONS!

"My husband and I were concerned about our ability to care for more than three children. We weren't sure how we could support more on a pastor's salary, and time and energy were in as short a supply as money. My husband did not want to see me go through another difficult pregnancy, and I was flattered by this concern for me. Our Christian friends were all very supportive of sterilization. We were even promised a better sex life if we did not have to 'worry' about getting pregnant!

"So, seven months after our third child was born, we made the decision for vasectomy. On the way to the hospital, however, I had an overwhelming sense that we should not go through with the procedure. We brushed it off as 'cold feet' but I know now that it was the voice of God speaking to my heart. The next day I started praying for a baby. I begged the Lord to heal my husband, to undo what we had done. I thought I was crazy; yet I knew that God had placed this longing in my heart.

"One day, after officiating at a baby dedication, my husband mentioned that it would be fun to have a baby in the house again. This was a green light to approach the subject in earnest. My husband started searching the Word and realized that children are a gift from the Lord and that he was a hypocrite if he failed to live that out in his life. We started shopping around for a doctor. The doctor asked my husband if he had had a change of wives! 'No,' he said, 'just a change of convictions!'

"After waiting for over two years, we eventually conceived and were blessed with a precious baby girl."

ARE YOU INTERESTED IN A REVERSAL?

Would you like to read more stories of those who have had reversals? Write for the book: *A Change of Heart: Fifty Testimonies of Couples Who Have Had Reversals from Vasectomies and Tubal Ligations*. Available for $12.00, plus shipping. Contact Above Rubies, P.O. Box 681687, Franklin, TN 37068-1687, www.aboverubies.org.

QUESTIONS

1. What do you think it means to allow God's sovereignty in our lives?

   _____

   _____

   _____

2. Read Romans 12:1-2 again. What does this Scripture mean to you in the light of yielding your fertility to the Lord?

   _____

   _____

   _____

3. Many times we are fearful of letting God control our lives. We like to have our hands on the reins. Name some

of the fears in your life that are a hindrance to trusting in God's sovereign will for your life.

_____

_____

_____

4. Confess these fears to the Lord and ask Him to deliver you. If you are studying this together in a group, pray for one another.

CHAPTER 15

*T*HE VISION

The fact of the matter is this: It is not a matter of our deciding how many children we should have, or should not have, but having a vision of God's plan for marriage and family—a vision to bring forth a godly seed for God's glory.

It is interesting to note that, in so many instances in the Word of God, that God gave the vision for family before children ever arrived on the scene. God wants us to have a vision for family, not just when we start a family, but also even before we are married. We should plant a vision for family in our children as they are growing up. We should train our sons to be fathers and therefore the providers, the protectors, and the priests of their homes. We should train and give our daughters a vision for motherhood, preparing them to be the nurturers, the nourishers, and the nest builders of future families. Let's look at some examples:

To All Mothers:

Genesis 3:20, "And Adam called his wife's name Eve: because she was the mother of all living." Just a minute. Let's look a little closer at this Scripture. At the time this was written, Eve was not yet a mother. She did not know anything about motherhood. She had never even seen a newborn baby. Adam had never seen his wife "with child" or seen a baby come forth from the womb. They had never seen a little child grow from a baby into adulthood. They had no experience in parenting children. So why is Adam calling Eve a mother when he knows nothing about the career of motherhood? Adam was speaking under the unction of the Holy One. He spoke forth a prophetic destiny over his wife, Eve, and over all women to come—that God's highest purpose for women was to be a *mother*. The destiny for women was spoken forth before motherhood was ever embarked upon. God gave the vision before the experience.

To Abraham:

God gave a vision to Abraham and he believed it. We read about it in Genesis 15:5-6, "He brought him forth abroad, and said, Look now toward heaven, and tell the stars, if thou be able to number them: and he said unto him, So shall thy seed be. And he believed in the Lord; and he counted it to him for righteousness."

Abraham did not believe God for only one son. He believed God for a family as many as the stars of heaven. He embraced the vision. He believed it when as yet he had no children.

To Sarah:

God gave Sarah a promise for motherhood while she was yet barren. Genesis 17:15-16, "And God said... I will bless her, and give thee a son also of her: yea, I will bless her, and she shall be a mother of nations; kings of people shall be of her."

To Rebekah:

In Genesis 24, we read the story of how Abraham sent his servant to find a bride for his son, Isaac. We know the lovely story of how Rebekah was chosen. Before she left to go to her new husband, her family pronounced a blessing upon her. As they did this, they gave her a vision for motherhood. It was not a little vision, but a big vision. Genesis 24:60, "And they blessed Rebekah, and said unto her, Thou art our sister, be thou the mother of thousands of millions, and let thy seed possess the gate of those which hate them."

To Jacob:

God gave a vision to Jacob and he believed it. We read about it in Genesis 28:10-22, "He dreamed, and behold a ladder set up on the earth, and the top of it reached to heaven: and behold the angels of God ascending and descending on it. And, behold, the Lord stood above it, and said, I am the Lord

God of Abraham thy father, and the God of Isaac: the land whereon thou liest, to thee will I give it, and to thy seed; and thy seed shall be as the dust of the earth, and thou shalt spread abroad to the west, and to the east, and to the north, and to the south: and in thee and in thy seed shall all the families of the earth be blessed."

We are familiar with the story of the angels of God ascending and descending on the ladder, but we forget the most important part of this dream. It was the message God gave to Jacob. It was a dream for his future life. And when did Jacob receive this dream? While he was still a single man. He did not even have a girlfriend! All he could think of was escaping the anger of his brother, Esau. Yes, even before he was married, God gave him a vision for a family. It wasn't for a little family, but a *big* family! As many as the dust of the earth. This is when young people should be given the vision for family, not waiting until they are married.

To the Children of Israel:

God promised to the children of Israel the blessing of multiplication through their fathers, Abraham, Isaac, and Jacob. Genesis 35:11,12 says, "I am God Almighty: be fruitful and multiply; a nation and a company of nations shall be of thee, and kings shall come out of thy loins; and the land which I gave Abraham and Isaac, to thee I will give it, and to thy seed after thee will I give the land." They believed it and became a great nation.

To Us:

We do not have to wait until we are married to get a vision for a family. We do not have to wait until we are married to decide whether we will have children. We enter into marriage with this purpose and vision. We have a dream. We have a dream to have the children God has planned for us to have. We lift up our eyes from the shortsighted humanistic agenda of 1.8 children per family to God's vision of filling the earth with His glory. We claim the promise of Psalm 112:1-2, "Blessed is the man who fears the Lord, who delights greatly in His commandments. His descendants will be mighty on earth; the generation of the upright will be blessed." The Hebrew word "mighty" is *gibbor* which means "warrior, one who excels, a champion, a mighty, valiant man." Oh what a vision—to invade the earth with mighty sons and daughters who have been trained and prepared for God's divine purposes.

The Muslim families of the world are not limiting their families. They have an average of 6.8 children per family and are the fastest growing religion in the world through their birth rate! In 1950, the industrial democracies of the world were twenty-two percent of the world's population. If we continue the present trend, we will only be five percent at the end of this century! The Western world that we know today will no longer be the same. Proverbs 14:28 (NLT) says, "A growing population is a king's glory; a dwindling nation is his doom."

It certainly is time to line up with God's vision. In fact, we are currently experiencing a dearth in the Christian world.

We do not see a harvest of souls coming into the kingdom. Oh yes, here and there—but not a great harvest. Once again, I feel that this hinges on our resistance to children from our loins. I believe that when we, as the church of God, repent for stopping the godly seed from coming into the world and begin to embrace life, that once again we will begin to see a harvest of souls being born-again into God's kingdom.

This vision is not just for the present, but also for the future. We trust God in His plan—that our children, our grandchildren, our great-grandchildren, and our future generations will fill the earth with His light and truth. What greater vision could we have? What greater way could we serve our living God?

QUESTIONS

1. Write down the vision you have for raising a family.

    _____

    _____

    _____

2. Explain how your vision is in line with God's Word.

    _____

    _____

    _____

3. Why is it important for young people to have a vision for raising a family before they get married?

    _____

    _____

    _____

4. Read Genesis 28:16-17. What was Jacobs's response when God told him He would multiply him greatly?

    _____

    _____

    _____

CHAPTER 16

$\mathcal{D}$O NOT DEPRIVE

When we refuse to have more children, we deprive many people. We deprive:

1. *God* This is the most serious. We deprive Him of the purposes and plans that He has for the children that He destined to be born.

2. *Eternity*. God wants to fill His house. He not only wants to fill the earth, but He wants to fill His eternal kingdom. We fill eternity with those who are born on earth.

3. *Ourselves*. We deprive ourselves of being blessed by God. Every child is another blessing. Once we receive the blessing of a child from God, we wonder how we could ever live without that child. When Onan destroyed his sperm, he was deprived of being in the lineage of Jesus. Judah then received this privilege in his place.

4. *Grandparents.* We deprive our parents of their "glory and honor" which are grandchildren. Read Proverbs 17:6. The Living Bible translation says, "An old man's grandchildren are his crowning glory." Why should we deprive our parents of their reward and glory in their older age?

5. *Our Children.* We deprive our present children of more brothers and sisters. Children love to have more children in the family. They love to have another baby brother or sister. I often sadly think of the brothers and sisters that I could have had. More brothers and sisters are always a blessing. If my parents had been willing to have more children, not only would I be more blessed, but also my children would have more uncles and aunts. If my siblings had trusted God for more children, my children would be blessed with more cousins, and I would have more nieces and nephews. Remember, God wants our families to be "like a flock."

6. *The Church.* The church today would be fifty to one-hundred percent stronger if we, the people of God, had not limited the godly seed. There would be more apostles, prophets, pastors, teachers, and evangelists.

7. *The World.* We deprive the world of the blessings of a godly seed. We deprive the world of being illuminated with light. We deprive the world of being "salted!" We deprive the world of more godly young people and men and women. We deprive the world of more godly mothers and fathers who will build strong families that will build a strong nation.

QUESTIONS

1. Write down those whom you have deprived by refusing to have children.

   _____

   _____

   _____

2. Write down the ways they have missed out.

   _____

   _____

   _____

3. In what way have you yourself been deprived?

   _____

   _____

   _____

CHAPTER 17

*W*HY PARENTS IN THE TWENTY-FIRST CENTURY LOVE HAVING CHILDREN

Ireceive constant complaints from mothers telling me how hurt they are from the negative comments they receive from family and friends when they share the news that they are going to have another baby. "God gave you a brain, didn't He?" or "Oh no, not another one!" and so on. One *Above Rubies* reader wrote to me, "…I cannot understand why people think children are such burdens that they'd only want one or two, and then suggest to me that I stop at that number also. I've sometimes joked with my husband that I could write a book of all the one-liners people say and title it, '101 Reasons Why Not to Have Any More Children.'"

This gave me a wonderful idea. However, I decided to dwell on the positive rather than the negative. I asked mothers all over America to share why they love having children. I received a wonderful response, so here are "101 Reasons Why

Mothers Love Having Children." Many of these reasons were reiterated over and over again by different mothers.

1. We love receiving gifts and blessings from God.

2. Why would I ever want to turn down one of God's blessings?

3. We not only want to receive gifts from God for ourselves, but we want to give more gifts to the world. Every child God gives us is a gift to the world.

4. It is so exciting to see whom God will send to bless us each time.

5. I am honored for the Lord to use my womb again.

6. I love being "with child."

7. I love to see what God thinks of next. I believe each child is a precious and unique thought, with vast possibilities, straight from our Heavenly Father. It is the most exciting thing in my entire life to give birth and see the new little person. There is nothing that moves me as much as seeing the birth of a baby.

8. I love to behold the handiwork of the Lord as a new little miracle comes forth.

9. The birth of a baby is the ultimate fulfillment of love between a husband and wife. Each child is an unbreakable bond between a father and mother.

10. It is amazing to think that each child is a part of my beloved husband and me.

11. God said to Jeremiah, "*Before* I formed you in the womb I knew you...." God is the One who will form my future children. If He knew Jeremiah before conception, then He knows all my children before conception; yes, even the children who haven't yet been formed. I don't want to refuse children God has chosen.

12. I'd love another baby because to choose not to is like saying "no" to God. I want to say "yes" to God and His will for my life.

13. I'll have more people to love.

14. I'll have more hands to help.

15. I'll have more babies to nurse and therefore less risk of breast cancer.

16. I feel so blessed that God wants to reward us again.

17. I look upon each child as an incredibly beautiful jewel. Each one takes on a different loveliness and I cannot wait to see the next jewel arrive.

18. Another baby in the family makes my other children so happy.

19. I love to see the faces of my children as they see a new brother or sister for the first time.

20. Babies teach the older children so much about caring for little ones, being kind, protective, and unselfish.

21. Children brighten up the home. They make life interesting.

22. I become a better mother with each child I have.

23. Children teach me patience.

24. My children think I'm beautiful no matter how I look.

25. The more children we have, the more they entertain one another.

26. There's always someone around to visit with, play with, pray with, or read to.

27. It is just as easy to cook for ten as it is for one!

28. More children give us the opportunity to have our faith increased as we see God meet our daily needs.

29. You have your own cheering squad in whatever you do.

30. The more children we have, the more impact we have upon the world.

31. We want to establish a godly dynasty that will continue down the generations to come.

32. We want to raise another soul for Jesus.

33. We desire to raise up a standard for God in this evil day.

34. More children releases more of Christ in our home.

35. Because babies are the most irresistible things on earth.

36. There is nothing like a new baby in the house.

37. There is no occupation more rewarding than motherhood.

38. Because I am fulfilling the only career that is eternal! Every other career will be left behind when we leave this earth, but I can take my children with me into glory. My children are eternal souls who will live forever.

39. Parenthood is investing in eternity.

40. Children are like arrows who we send to places where we will never be able to go.

41. We want to fill our quiver.

42. Because of the people who might be reached for Christ through this child.

43. I want to increase the "salt" and "light" proportion in the world!

44. We're forming our own orchestra to make music to the Lord.

45. Having and raising children aids in sanctification of us parents.

46. Having children helps to develop in us the godly character of servanthood.

47. My children help me surrender the selfish desires of my flesh.

48. Parenthood allows us to experience the kind of love our Heavenly Father has for us.

49. In an era when so many individuals condone the denial or taking of life—we want to give life—for life is sacred.

50. We don't want to deprive our parents of their "crowning glory" (Proverbs 17:6). We want to bless them with grandchildren.

51. Our children are my teachers. I learn sweet things from them every day.

52. I'm replenishing the earth with godly seed.

53. I want to be obedient to God's Word to "Be fruitful and multiply."

54. My children are my friends and my brothers and sisters in the Lord. Now who can have too many of these?

55. I have a passionate love for babies.

56. I just love being a mother. I love being pregnant. I love giving birth and I love breastfeeding.

57. I love the sweet smiles, the delightful giggle, and the soft baby to cuddle.

58. Jesus said that when we welcome a little child into our home and family, we are actually welcoming Him. I don't want to spurn Jesus.

59. We want our children to have the riches of many relationships with brothers and sisters. When we are no longer living, our children will have each other for encouragement, fellowship, and a sense of family.

60. The more children we have, the more our love is multiplied.

61. We still have an empty seat in our van, and we'd like to fill it!

62. Our children are all so wonderful, who could resist another one?

63. God says that children are a reward and we believe Him!

64. Children are the most precious gift of marriage.

65. We get lots of experience in sharing and communicating.

66. Children help me see my daily dependence on God for His wisdom and strength.

67. I love to feel a precious life within my womb.

68. Large families are *fun*! And we love having fun.

69. In a large family, the children and teenagers don't want to go out to find entertainment because they are lonely and bored—there is already fun and entertainment at home.

70. A new baby reminds me of how Jesus came into the world.

71. To be open to more children shows our present children that we love them. How can our children understand the love of God if we have the attitude that a certain number of children is too many?

72. More children help to grow the church.

73. I want to rear strong soldiers for the Lord.

74. My body was created for this purpose.

75. Family celebrations—birthdays, holidays, and Christmas— are even more wonderful with a new baby in the house.

76. Hope for mankind is expressed in the miracle of a baby's birth. Wherever there is life, there is hope.

77. Babies are sweet, cuddly, and adorable and have so much potential. It is like planting seeds in a flower garden—a beautiful bouquet for the future.

78. There will be more people to pay for the aged's social security benefits.

79. I want to yield my womb as a living sacrifice to God.

80. To prevent menses and enjoy the nursing hormones of prolactin and oxytocin. My most enjoyable and peaceful times are during the absence of menses during pregnancy.

81. Babies remind us of how wonderful and how creative our God is.

82. We are training a godly generation that will cover the earth with the Gospel and prepare the way for Jesus' return.

83. Younger children teach the older children how to be helpers. By the time they are old enough to be married and have children of their own, they'll be prepared for raising them.

84. I want another arrow for God's army.

85. I love to feel a precious new life moving within me.

86. I would hate to stand before God on Judgment Day and have to answer why I rejected the children He had ordained for our family.

87. Our children have taught me the value of relationships and the shallowness of the world's value system.

88. I trust God in all other areas of my life and I want to trust Him in the area of having children, too.

89. It sure is nice to kiss and smell a little one again. Their scent is so sweet.

90. Babies are also a blessing to other people. They sure love to hold and cuddle mine. Since my siblings have stopped at two children per family, I want to supply them for my parents and everyone else's pleasure.

91. Our horizon and interests are constantly widened. Each child is born with a different destiny upon his or her life. Each child has different gifts. As we encourage our children in their varied gifts, we constantly learn new things ourselves. Our children will often take on ventures and interests that we would never have dreamed of. Parenthood is not confining, but enlarging.

92. Babies are future dishwashers!

93. Babies are a lot more entertaining than television.

94. We're helping to build the kingdom of God.

95. So I can buy cute baby and children's clothes, even if it is at a yard sale.

96. I'll be able to spend eternity with my children.

97. Children teach me to become a servant, and that's what Jesus wants us to be. Jesus Himself said He came to serve rather than to be served.

98. To be convicted of sin and the need for repentance as I observe my sinful nature in my children's sinful natures.

99. The more children we have, the more we will be blessed when we are older. Instead of being lonely, we will have many children and grandchildren around to entertain us, to bless us, and to care for us.

100. Raising up a godly seed is laying up treasure in heaven.

101. Having children causes us to depend upon God moment by moment!

*W*HAT DO CHILDREN SAY?

A fter receiving wonderful comments from mothers all over the nation, I thought it would be great to hear how children would respond if asked, "Why would you like another brother or sister?" I therefore asked mothers to ask this question to their children. Here are some of their comments:

Two Years Old:

"'Cause we not have any baby no more. Reuben's a big boy now!" (This is Reuben talking!)

Three Years Old:

"I hold her gently and I read her a great story. She will love it. I would tell her she's my favorite little girl, ever!" (There are no girls in this family, yet!)

"I would sing him a baby lullaby song."

"I would rock him to sleep."

"I'd like a baby brother, because I want to see him in my belly." (Already wanting to become a mommy!)

"More to play hide and seek with me."

"'Cause I love him and I want to hold him."

"Because they smile and they hold your fingers."

Four Years Old:

"So I can play with them."

"Cuz I like them so much."

"So I can play with him on my bunk bed."

"Because I love my brothers and sisters."

"I like them to grow up with me."

Five Years Old:

"I would love us to have another baby. I think babies are so soft, sweet, and so squishy."

"I love to play with them and kiss them."

"I really, *really* like them. I feel so happy when I have a new little baby." (After this answer, this young boy, eyes shining in anticipation, asked his mother, "So Mama, why are you askin'? Are you havin' another baby for us?")

"I want three baby brothers because Daddy's the only boy."

"I want a baby brother so Elijah won't fight over Naomi when I want to hold her." (They have a six-week-old baby in this home, but obviously one baby is not enough!)

"I just feel like having one so I can name one Little Foot. I like playing
with babies, too."

"I would take care of him and love him like a mom."

"Because I want to change his nappies and have a bath with him."

Six Years Old:

"Because I love babies."

"Because I want to hug another one. And I could babysit at home."

"I could make him laugh and teach him how to do tricks and how to play games."

Seven Years Old:

"I love babies because their skin is so soft."

"I want to see a miracle of God."

"Babies are fun to play with each day."

"I love babies. They are so cute."

"So that I can learn to love and care for them."

"Because children are a blessing from God."

"We want a family soccer team."

"Because there would be five instead of four." (Children always want one more, no matter how many in the family.

Eight Years Old:

"I would like another baby to have more friends. The more children we have, the funnier it is. When I grow up, I want at least a thousand babies!"

Nine Years Old:

"Mummy, I want you to keep having babies forever because they're so cute!"

"Because God said, 'Be fruitful and multiply.'"

"I like to babysit them, take care of them, and play with them. I like to dress them up and pick out their clothes."

"More friends to have compassion on."

Ten Years Old:

Written at the top of a Christmas list: "A new brother or sister." There were already ten children in the family at this time.

"I would love another baby to snuggle it. I love having a baby in the house."

"Babies are very cute."

"So I can have some company to play with."

"I would like a bigger family with more brothers and sisters to play with."

"I want a baby brother. I've always wanted one since I was little and I'm tired of sisters and their Barbies!"

"Because when they are babies they are really cute and funny. When they get bigger and older they are fun to play with. I like to help them do things and learn things."

Eleven Years Old:

"I was so happy I started to cry." (On hearing the news her mother was having a baby.)

"I can't wait to play with him and take him to the park when he is older."

Twelve Years Old:

"I want a lot of babies so I can learn how to be a father."

"I want a new baby so I can share my room with someone else."

"Babies are a gift and we should accept them with love and care."

"It is such a good feeling to rock a baby to sleep."

Thirteen Years Old:

"Babies are so sweet to cuddle."

Fourteen Years Old:

"I would love more babies so I can care for them, dress, and change them."

"I love to laugh at their cute antics."

"When the baby grows up, I could show him things and teach him."

The most frequent comment from children, which was repeated over and over again by nearly every child, was "So that I can play with them." Children love company. They love to have another brother or sister to play with. They get bored on their own. They would rather have another brother or sister than the newest and most expensive toy you could buy them. A new baby becomes a friend for life.

Children learn their social skills by playing with one another and with different age groups. It was never God's intention for children to be separated by age group, as is the format for public schools. If children can only play with those of their own age group, they are limited in their social skills. Children learn best by playing with different age groups— older and younger children.

God also sets the solitary in families. As it is not good for man to be alone, it is also not good for a child to be an "only child." Every child longs to have company, and the more the better. In fact, many mothers with only one child don't realize that it is actually easier to care for two or more children than one child. The more you have, the easier it is. I found it easier when I had my sixth baby (even though I had five others to care for) than I did with my first. As you continue to have more children, the older children are able to not only play with, but also help care for, the younger children. There are more hands to do the work. As the whole family works together to build a strong family, the workload is spread amongst all. It becomes teamwork rather than one person trying to do it all.

There are some mothers who fear to have a second child because the first one is so time-consuming. But the first child is always the most time consuming because the mother is the baby's sole entertainer. When other children come along, they help to entertain the first child.

How can our children understand the love of God if we have the attitude that a certain number of children is too many?

One mother of eight children wrote to me, "The way to show the children you have that you love them, is to have more children. My husband was an only child and he always felt his parents did not want more children because he was too much trouble. How can our children understand the love of God if we have the attitude that a certain number of children is too many? Many people think they're taking something away from their older children by having more, but our experience has been the opposite. They do not need more things, more entertainment, more clothes, better food, etc. They need parents who love them. They also need to learn to sacrifice for the good of all and to give up things for the younger and weaker siblings."

QUESTIONS FOR CHAPTERS 16 AND 17

1. From the "101 Reasons Why Mothers Love Having Children" that you have read, what is the reason that you like best, and why?

   _____

   _____

   _____

2. Can you think of another reason that is special to you?

   _____

   _____

   _____

3. Write down or share how your children are blessed by their brothers and sisters?

   _____

   _____

   _____

4. Share why you found it was easier to rear succeeding children than your first child.

_____

_____

_____

ABOUT THE AUTHOR

Nancy Campbell is mother to six and grandmother to twenty-one. She serves her husband Colin Campbell (a pastor of many years) as a helpmeet, wife, and mother, but also through a special "Titus 2" ministry to ladies. For more than twenty six years, her *Above Rubies* magazine has reached thousands of women in America, New Zealand, and Australia, communicating a message of virtuous womanhood. This magazine goes to over ninety countries of the world and has a current circulation of over 100,000. It is financed by the donations of its readers and those who have a burden to see the restoration of family life in the nation. Nancy and Colin moved to Australia in 1982 and then to America in 1991, and now reside in Primm Springs, Tennessee.

ALSO BY THE AUTHOR

The Power of Motherhood:
What the Bible Says About Mothers

This manual is guaranteed to strengthen, fortify, inspire, and encourage you in your high calling of motherhood.

The Family Meal Table and Hospitality

This manual will give you a vision for your family meal table far beyond what you have ever dreamed.

If you would like to receive the *Above Rubies* magazine or order the manuals, contact:

Above Rubies
P.O. Box 681687
Franklin, TN 37068-1687
USA
E-mail: nancy@aboverubies.org
Web page: www.aboverubies.org

Nancy Campbell also writes a Weekly E-mail Devotion to encourage women. To receive this, send a blank e-mail to: subscribers-on@aboverubies.org.

Colin Campbell writes a bi-weekly message for men. To receive this, send a blank e-mail to: menslist-on@aboverubies.org.